CULTURES OF THE WORLD
ITALY
3rd ed.

Cavendish
Square
New York

Published in 2014 by Cavendish Square Publishing, LLC
303 Park Avenue South, Suite 1247, New York, NY 10010

Third Edition

This publication is published with arrangement with Marshall Cavendish International (Asia) Pte Ltd.

Copyright © 2014 Marshall Cavendish International (Asia) Pte Ltd.

Website: cavendishsq.com

Cultures of the World is a registered trademark of Times Publishing Limited.

This publication represents the opinions and views of the author based on his or her personal experience, knowledge, and research. The information in this book serves as a general guide only. The author and publisher have used their best efforts in preparing this book and disclaim liability rising directly or indirectly from the use and application of this book.

CPSIA Compliance Information: Batch #WS13CSQ

All websites were available and accurate when this book was sent to press.

Library of Congress Cataloging-in-Publication Data
Winter, Jane Kohen, 1959–
    Italy / Jane Kohen Winter, Leslie Jermyn, Jo-Ann Spilling. — 3rd ed.
        p. cm. — (Cultures of the world)
    Includes bibliographical references and index.
    Summary: Provides comprehensive information on the geography, history, wildlife, governmental structure, economy, cultural diversity, peoples, religion, and culture of Malaysia"—Provided by publisher.
    ISBN 978-1-60870-870-3 (print) – ISBN 978-1-60870-876-5 (ebook)
    1. Italy—Juvenile literature. I. Jermyn, Leslie. II. Spilling, Jo-Ann.
III. Title. IV. Series.

DG417.W56 2014
    945—dc23   2012018492

Writers: Jane Kohen Winter, Leslie Jermyn, Jo-Ann Spilling
Editors: Deborah Grahame-Smith, Mindy Pang
Copyreader: Tara Tomczyk
Designers: Nancy Sabato, Adithi
Cover picture researcher: Tracey Engel
Picture researcher: Joshua Ang

PICTURE CREDITS
Cover: © theodore liasi / Alamy
Corbis / Click Photos 28, 112 • Getty Images 73 • Inmagine 1, 3, 5, 6, 8, 10, 13, 14, 15, 16, 18, 20, 21, 24, 26, 27, 29, 30, 32, 33, 34, 37, 38, 40, 41, 42, 43, 44, 45, 46, 47, 48, 49, 50, 51, 52, 53, 54, 55, 56, 58, 59, 60, 61, 62, 64, 65, 67, 69, 71, 72, 74, 75, 76, 78, 79, 80, 81, 82, 83, 84, 86, 87, 88, 89, 90, 91, 93, 94, 96, 97, 99, 100, 101, 102, 103, 104, 105, 107, 108, 109, 110, 111, 114, 115, 116, 117, 118, 119, 120, 122, 123, 124, 125, 126, 127, 128, 129, 130, 131 • North Wind Picture Archives 23 • Wikimedia Commons 92, 95, 98

PRECEDING PAGE
A winding rural road near the picturesque town of Monticchiello in Val d'Orcia, Tuscany.

Printed in the United States of America

CONTENTS

ITALY TODAY

SINCE ANCIENT TIMES, WHEN THE ROMAN EMPIRE RULED MOST of Western Europe from its base in the city of Rome, Italy has exerted great influence in the advancement of Europe and Western civilization. Today Italy is one of the largest economies in the world and continues to play a significant role in the development of the European Union.

As a peninsula extending into the central Mediterranean Sea, Italy is easily recognized by its boot-like shape. This nation-state consists of an interesting and varied mix of geographical features. It is dominated by mountains—the northern Dolomite mountain range and the Apennine, which extends from the north to the south, slicing through the center of the country. Just south of the Dolomites, there is the fertile agricultural land of the Po Valley. Italy is also made up of two large islands—the mountainous Sardinia and the volcanic Sicily. Within Italy there exist two sovereign states—Vatican City, where the Pope generally resides, and the oldest surviving Republic of San Marino.

Italy offers many attractions; its cultural and historical heritage is a magnet to tourists—more than 43 million visitors arrive every year from all over the

Gondolas gliding along the iconic Grand Canal in the watery Italian city of Venice.

globe, making it the fifth most visited country in the world. The tourism industry is a key contributor to Italy's economy, generating vital revenue and providing much-needed employment opportunities for many, particularly in the service sector. Tourists come to experience Italy's ancient history, famous artworks, fine cuisine, and spectacular scenery. Popular places to visit include the unique Leaning Tower of Pisa, the waterways and gondolas of Venice, the Colosseum and other ancient ruins and monuments in Rome, the splendid Ponte Vecchio in Florence, the vineyards and medieval hill towns of Tuscany, the stunning coastline along the Amalfi coast, the alpine ski resorts of the Dolomites and much more.

More than 70 percent of Italy's population (of more than 61 million) live in cities and towns while the rest of the people live in rural areas. It is a well-known fact that within Italy there exists a distinct North-South divide. Northern Italy is prosperous. It enjoys a developed and industrialized economy, producing and manufacturing the best designs in clothing, textiles, footwear, furniture, cars, and electronics. The North also produces agricultural items including wheat, rice, and grain. Southern Italy is comparatively poorer—its economy is less advanced, with many working on farms and growing fruits and vegetables.

In northern Italy the climate can be extremely cold in the winter months, with temperatures plummeting below freezing levels with snowfall in many areas. In contrast southern Italy has a milder and generally warmer climate; certain parts of the south can be extremely hot and dry in the height of summer.

The pace of living in the North is more hectic, while in the South there is a more relaxed approach to life. Apart from the differences in wealth and climate, many believe there are also differences in the characteristics of the people in the North and those from the South. Those in the North of Italy often think of Southerners as idle and lacking in ambition. Unsurprisingly Southerners think that their northern counterparts take work far too seriously and are unable to enjoy life.

Italy ranks among the top most expensive European Union countries to live in. Italy has one of the highest rates of home ownership in the world, at roughly 78 percent, and Italians often buy their homes outright, with help from their families, rather than take out loans. Italians living in urban areas generally endure a higher cost of living. Living in the larger northern cities such as Rome and Milan can be considerably more costly than living in the more rural southern towns and villages. Although the cost of living is lower in the southern parts of the country, many Southerners choose to live in the industrialized North because there are more opportunities for work, although most harbor plans to return to the South when they can afford to.

Italian taxes rank among the highest in the world. The cost of living is further increased by the numerous taxes present in almost all forms, from minor purchases to major expenditures such as housing and employment. In recent years Italy has experienced rising inflation at a steady rate—from 1997 to 2010 the average inflation rate was 2.2 percent, peaking at 4.1 percent in 2008.

Estimated monthly cost of housing for a single person is approximately 400 euros ($518) including utilities and water. The standard type of housing unit is an apartment comprising two to four bedrooms, costing around 2,500 euros ($3,235) every month. Many affluent families live in lavish condominiums that can cost around 10,000 euros ($12,941) per month. These are normally located in the center of cities and towns and also along the coast. Those who live in the more rural and remote areas live on farmland in cottages or villas.

In recent years Italy has been described as "the sick man of Europe," referring to the country's struggle to improve its structural and political problems, which many believe prevent the country from overcoming its economic woes. The financial crisis of 2008 forced Italy, together with several other countries in Europe, to tighten its belt with regard to public spending. Encumbered with a massive public debt, fragile public finances, uncertain economic growth, and burdened by an aging population that constitutes almost 20 percent of the total population, the Italian government has had to implement various severe and unfavorable austerity measures—including one of the least popular initiatives, freezing public sector salaries—in order to battle the current economic slowdown. To add to the economic crisis it faces, Italy suffers from the existence of the underground and often illegal activities of the notorious mafia, which not only drains off money from the real economy, but also promotes uncertainty and suspicion among investors

Sheep grazing on the Alps mountains in South Tyrol.

and others in the business sector. As is the case elsewhere in Europe, in Italy there is, at present, widespread dissatisfaction with government policies among the people as unemployment soars to record levels and social problems rise.

Although millions of Italians are facing challenging economic problems, it is important to recognize that the Italians of the past have left an indelible mark, shaping the beliefs and lifestyles of the population of Europe and around the world through their scientific discoveries and inventions as well as their explorations in the spheres of art and literature. Famous scientists and inventors include Galileo Galilee and Leonardo da Vinci. Celebrated artists include Michelangelo and Dante Alighieri.

Many contemporary Italians continue to follow in the prominent footsteps of their ancestors by making valuable contributions to the arts and science. A few world-renowned Italians today include film director Federico Fellini, fashion designers Giorgio Armani and Gianni Versace, motor-racing driver and sports car manufacturer Enzo Ferrari, and international superstar tenor Luciano Pavarotti.

Apart from these eminent Italians, ordinary Italians, both young and old, possess a passion for life and a love for simple pleasures. These simple pleasures, including spending time with the family and taking pride in the creation of good food and wine, make up the fabric and foundation of traditional Italian life.

The average Italian spends around 200 euros ($259) on food and drink every month. Although Italians enjoy socializing around food, many are aware that the cost of eating out is variable depending on where one chooses to eat. Family-run restaurants can charge one person 50 to 100 euros ($65 to $129), while luxury fine-dining establishments can charge up to 300 euros ($388) for a three-course meal.

Italians are fortunate that many acres of arable farmland are given to producing delicious tomatoes, potatoes, carrots, bell peppers, herbs, fruit, almonds and hazelnuts, coffee, and much more. Italy also produces high-quality cheese, extra virgin olive oil, pasta, and meat products. However, a large proportion of this desirable produce is widely exported to other countries in Europe, America, Asia, and beyond, where they can be sold for higher prices. Sadly local produce is no longer affordable to everyone, in particular the poorer Italians.

Italy's love affair with food has permeated almost every corner of the globe, and Italian cuisine, in particular pasta and pizza, can be easily found in almost any restaurant in any city or town in the world. Similarly Italian coffee culture—espressos, lattes, and cappuccinos—is now becoming a common feature of daily life for many people across different parts of the world.

Apart from food, fashion is another passion among the Italians. Italian style and couture is internationally acclaimed and celebrated. Its famous designers and fashion labels—Armani, Versace, Gucci, Prada, Dolce and Gabbana, Missoni, Ferragamo, Miu Miu, Roberto Cavalli—offer the world's best when it comes to luxury fashion. Designers from London, New York, Paris, and Tokyo flock annually to Italy's fashion capital of Milan to view runway shows and attend fashion events that showcase the latest in seasonal trends. Italian fashion is most admired for its classic, elegant lines and flawless craftsmanship.

Italy offers both local and international customers the finest in fashion accessories, including shoes, handbags, and suitcases. Many of the world's famous fashion houses are headquartered in Milan, making significant contributions to the Italian economy as a whole. In 2008 the clothing and textile industry contributed approximately 26.7 percent to the country's GDP, while the footwear sector, on its own, provided almost 5 percent.

Although the famous fashion labels are available in all the major cities, only the very wealthy can afford to indulge in these luxury items. The average Italian spends around 200 euros ($259) a month on clothing, although the more affluent with a more generous budget will perhaps spend thousands of euros every month. While tourists and the rich patronize luxury designer stores, ordinary Italians purchase their items of clothing and accessories at department stores and flea markets.

In spite of the economic and social trials and tribulations prevailing in the country today, Italy and its people continue to strive for progress while staying rooted in their glorious past. It is this ability to embrace modernity with antiquity that makes this country vibrant.

GEOGRAPHY

Reflection of the Alpine mountains on a lake in the Fanes-Sennes-Prags Nature Park in South Tyrol.

1

Contoured
naturally as
a long, boot-
shaped peninsula
protruding into the
Mediterranean
Sea, Italy has
one of the most
recognizable
geographic shapes
in the world.

ITALY IS A LONG, thin peninsula that extends from the southern coast of Europe. Its immediate neighbors—France, Switzerland, Austria, and Slovenia—are in the north, where the Alps form a broad arc around the top edge of the country. Four seas water the long coastline of the Italian peninsula and islands.

Except in the north, Italy is surrounded by water. The country has a coastline of about 4,700 miles (7,600 kilometers), bordered by the Adriatic Sea to the east, the Ionian Sea to the south, the Tyrrhenian Sea to the west, and the Ligurian Sea to the northwest.

Italy has an area of about 116,348 square miles (301,340 square km), which makes it slightly larger than the U.S. state of Arizona. On a map the Italian peninsula resembles a tall boot extending into the Mediterranean Sea toward the northern coast of Africa, which, at its closest point is only about 90 miles (145 km) away. The peninsula is 170 miles (274 km) wide at its broadest point and 708 miles (1,140 km) long.

In addition to the peninsula, Italy also includes a number of islands; the largest two are Sicily and Sardinia. Sicily, with an area of 9,927 square miles (25,711 square km), is separated from mainland Italy by the Strait of Messina, which is less than 2 miles (3.2 km) wide. Sardinia has an area of 9,301 square miles (24,090 square km) and lies 160 miles (257 km) off the Italian coast in the Tyrrhenian Sea. Some of the smaller islands include Elba in the Tuscan Archipelago and Ischia off the coast of Naples.

Italy also has two small independent states within its borders—the Republic of San Marino at just 25 square miles (65 square km) and Vatican City, even smaller at only 0.17 square miles (0.44 square km).

MOUNTAINS, LAKES, AND RIVERS

Italy is a mountainous country, and about a third of its landmass is above 2,500 feet (762 meters). Flat plains make up less than a quarter of the land. The two mountain ranges in Italy are the Alps and the Apennines. Italy's tallest mountains are in the Alps. Monte Bianco, the highest peak in Europe at 15,771 feet (4,805 m), lies on the Italian-French border; the Matterhorn, an Alpine peak at 14,692 feet (4,478 m), lies on the Italian-Swiss border.

The Dolomites in the eastern Italian Alps near Slovenia are so named because the terrain consists primarily of dolomite rock, a sedimentary rock found in many parts of the world. The Dolomites are extremely popular with skiers during the winter months.

At the foot of the Alps lie Italy's largest lakes: the 58-square-mile (150-square-km) Lake Como, the 82-square-mile (212-square-km) Lake Maggiore, and the 148-square-mile (383-square-km) Lake Garda. The western edge of the Alps is the source of Italy's most important river, the Po. The Po Valley is the principal plains region, Italy's flattest and most fertile stretch of land.

The Apennines divide Italy in two down its length, extending from the northwest of the country to the southern tip of the peninsula in the province of Calabria and then on to northern Sicily. The highest peak in the Apennines, at just under 10,000 feet (3,047 m), is Monte Corno, northeast of Rome.

NORTHERN ITALY

Italy's northern region consists of the Alps and the Po Valley. The mountains shield the Italian Riviera and the lake district from extreme temperatures. Here tourism is the most important industry. The largest city in the region is Genoa, the center of Italy's shipbuilding industry and the birthplace of Christopher Columbus.

The Po Valley stretches 280 miles (450 km) from Turin in the west to Udine in the east. The valley contains Italy's most productive farmland, much

The Apennine Range forms the very backbone of the Italian peninsula, running north to south through the country for 870 miles (1,400 km). The Apennines are not actually a single range of mountains; rather the name Apennines is given to a chain that links three smaller ranges together. The northern range is divided into the Ligurian and Umbrian Apennines, while the central range is divided into the Umbrian-Marchean and Abruzzi Apennines.

The ranges form an arc that divides the peninsula quite clearly into the eastern (Adriatic) and western coasts. The name is thought to originate from a fourth-century Celtic word, Penn, *which means "mountain" or "summit." The highest point in the range is the Corno Grande (Big Horn)* (shown in photo), *which reaches an elevation of 9,554 feet*

(2,912 m). The northern mountains are mostly covered with grass, while the southern section of the range is quite arid. Many of Italy's rare and endangered animals live in the Apennines, including bears, lynx, and wolves.

In the third century B.C. *the ancient Romans built a famous road, called the Via Flaminia, that crossed the Apennines to link Rome with the port of Ariminum (Rimini) on the Adriatic coast. Modern roads have since made crossing the mountains an easy task, but rare stretches of this ancient route can still be found today.*

of which is devoted to growing grains, especially rice, corn, and wheat. The Po Valley is also Italy's industrial center.

Venice, on the Adriatic Sea, is another very popular tourist center. Built on 118 islands, this romantic city is noted for its art and architecture. Milan, the capital of Lombardy and Italy's second-largest city, is located in the plains zone of Lombardy. The country's financial and commercial capital, Milan is Italy's richest city. Turin, the capital of Piedmont, is also an important business center and home to the famous Italian automobile makers Fabbrica Italiana di Automobili Torino (Fiat).

A villa sits atop a beautiful meadow in Asciano, a hill town in the province of Siena, in the region of Tuscany.

"A man who has not been in Italy, is always conscious of an inferiority, from his not having seen what it is expected a man should see."
—Samuel Johnson, 18th-century English writer

SOUTHERN ITALY

Southern Italy—consisting of the central and southern regions—is characterized by the rugged terrain of the Apennines. Land in the central region is not as fertile or well-irrigated as in the north. Nevertheless the area is dotted with small farms growing beans, wheat, olives, and the grapes used to produce Chianti wines.

The central southern region is home to the nation's capital, Rome, and Tuscany's capital, Florence, historically two of the most influential cities in Europe.

Rome has been the capital of modern Italy since 1870. The city's streets and piazzas (plazas) are lined with old buildings, graceful monuments, and magnificent statues and fountains. Within Rome is Vatican City, probably Italy's most visited site. The Vatican is the world center of the Roman Catholic Church and the home of the Pope.

Florence rivals Venice in architectural beauty. Florence's charming, winding streets open up into elegant piazzas filled with churches and their Renaissance treasures.

The most important city in southern Italy is Naples. Crammed with people, cars, factories, and refineries, it is the third-largest city in Italy and an important port.

Much of the land in the south is dry and yields little agricultural produce. However, certain areas of Campania have good soil, enriched by volcanic ash that produces excellent fruit and vegetables.

SICILY AND SARDINIA

Sicily is the largest and most beautiful of all Mediterranean islands. Most of its hilly terrain is used to cultivate wheat and beans and as grazing land for sheep. In the shadow of the active volcano Etna (the name is derived from the Greek word *aitho*, meaning "I burn"), tropical fruit trees thrive. The capital of Sicily is the port of Palermo, located on the Tyrrhenian Sea.

Sardinia has few good roads and a harsh, mountainous terrain that is mainly used for rearing sheep and growing wheat, olive trees, and grapevines where irrigation is possible. Sardinia's beautiful beaches are developed for international tourism. The capital of Sardinia is the port of Cagliari on the southern coast.

Whitewashed houses on one of the Aegadian Islands in Sicily.

CLIMATE

Most of Italy enjoys Mediterranean weather, with some climatic variation. Although it can get very cold in the Alpine areas in the winter, the peninsula generally experiences milder weather in the winters and much hotter summers, especially in the south.

In the plains the short winter can be harsh and the long summer hot. The coastal lowlands are warm even in winter. The highlands in the interior receive a lot of snow.

A hot wind, called the sciroc, blows over southern Italy in the summer, carrying fine sand from the Sahara Desert in North Africa. Sicily and Sardinia experience long, hot, and dry summers and relatively warm winters.

PLANTS

Beech trees, spruce, and other conifers populate the Italian Alps, while the lower altitudes are dominated by oak, chestnut, pine, and poplar. There are also maple, lime, elm, ash, birch, fir, and chestnut trees. Trees found in the northern lake district include evergreens, cork oak, cypress, and olive. Carob, red juniper, olive, almond, and citrus trees grow in central and southern Italy. The broom that grows around Etna is an endemic species of Sardinia.

ANIMAL LIFE

The Italian Alps are home to deer, wild goats, and a kind of antelope called chamois. Wild bears are found only in the regions of Abruzzi and Trentino—Alto Adige. Wildcats such as the lynx roam the Apennines, and wolves inhabit hills in the south.

EARTHQUAKES AND VOLCANOES

Italy has, for centuries, been vulnerable to volcanic eruptions and earthquakes. Regions in the Alps and Apennines have had their share of tremors and earthquakes, as have areas around Naples and in the regions of Umbria, Abruzzi, and Friuli—Venezia Giulia in the last 20 years. Among Italy's active volcanoes are Etna in Sicily and Vesuvius near Naples. One of the country's latest big earthquakes occurred in 1997 in Umbria and Marche. It killed 11 people, injured more than 100, and severely damaged the Basilica of Saint Francis of Assisi. In 2002 an earthquake of magnitude 5.6 hit Sicily, damaging some buildings, especially in the capital, Palermo. More recently, more than 300 people were killed in April 2009 when a powerful earthquake hit the central Italian town of L'Aquila.

Probably the most famous eruption in Italy, and one that has fascinated historians for centuries, was the eruption of Mount Vesuvius on August 24 in A.D. 79 that destroyed the Roman cities of Pompeii and Herculaneum. The eruption spewed huge amounts of ash and pumice into the sky and within three hours buried the city of Pompeii and the nearby town of Herculaneum under debris, lava, and mud.

Only in the late 19th century did archaeologists begin to uncover these ancient Roman cities. Incredibly they found that the carbon-rich ash had preserved many of the details of daily life in Pompeii. Entire bakeries were found with ovens containing loaves of bread still intact, as well as elegantly painted frescoes on bedroom walls, thousands of scrolls made from papyrus in libraries, statues, seedlings in gardens, and human skeletons. Graffiti on the walls of buildings could still be read.

In 2001 a team led by archaeologist Giuseppe Mastrolorenzo made a startling discovery about how some of the victims of the A.D. 79 eruption had died. Unlike the skeletons previously found, the 80 that Mastrolorenzo's team studied, found in boat sheds along the beach at Herculaneum, showed signs that it was not suffocation but intense heat that had killed those victims, vaporizing their flesh before they could even feel the incinerating heat!

Parts of Pompeii still lie buried. The cost of unearthing and preserving the cities' treasures is exorbitant and there are insufficient resources to finance preservation efforts.

Indigenous and migratory birds on the Italian peninsula and on the islands include herons, egrets, bitterns, gulls, terns, swallows, ospreys, harriers, owls, and warblers. Predatory birds include hawks, eagles, and crows. Teals, shovelers, and tufted ducks travel from northern Europe to winter in Italy. Other ducks found in Italy include the great crested grebe, water rail, coot, and moorhen. The Mediterranean Sea supports a variety of fish such as sardines, anchovies, squid, tuna, swordfish, perch, mullet, sharks, and mackerel. The largest otter population on the Italian peninsula lives at the foot of the Appenines in the Campania region.

Italian reptiles include the marsh tortoise, common toad, salamander, gecko, ululone (a yellow-bellied frog), and the poisonous Orsini's viper. Other regulars in Italy's wildlife scene include hedgehogs, porcupines, badgers, foxes, weasels, hares, wild boar, shrews, field mice, and bats.

"The Creator made Italy from designs by Michelangelo."
—19th-century American novelist Mark Twain.

INTERNET LINKS

www.boston.com/bigpicture/2009/04/the_laquila_earthquake.html

This website from the *Boston Globe* contains a picture story showing scenes from the earthquake that destroyed the Italian town of L'Aquila in 2009.

http://riverandchildren.pbworks.com

This bilingual English and Italian educational site includes questions, facts, and photographs of Italy's longest river, Po.

www.guardian.co.uk/science/2010/mar/31/toads-detect-earthquakes-study

Research showing that toads predicted the 2009 L'Aquila earthquake.

www.parks.it/parco.nazionale.abruzzo/Epar.php

This site provides data, facts, and photographs of one of Italy's best-known national parks, Parco Nazionale d'Abruzzo, in Lazio e Molise.

HISTORY

The Colosseum in Rome was built in the first century A.D. at the height of the Roman Empire. According to historical records, 50,000 spectators could watch gladiators fight wild beasts or other gladiators.

2

A LTHOUGH THE ITALIAN REPUBLIC has been in existence for just over 150 years, Italian history goes back to at least one thousand years before the birth of Christ. The history of Italy can be traced during the centuries through the different civilizations and empires that once claimed parts of the land—Etruscans, Greeks, Carthaginians, Norman French, Germans, Austrians, Aragonese Spanish, and the Roman Catholic Church.

THE ETRUSCANS AND THE PHOENICIANS

Peoples speaking Indo-European languages settled on the Italian peninsula as early as the 16th century B.C. Around 1100 B.C., the Villanovan people came to northern Italy from central Europe, while between 1100 and 700 B.C. the Illyrians migrated from the Balkans to central and southern Italy.

The Etruscans had a strong influence on early Roman society. The origins of the Etruscans are lost in history, but the first Etruscans are thought to have arrived in Italy around 1200 B.C. Historians believe that they came from Lydia, an ancient kingdom in present-day Turkey. The Etruscans spoke their own language and had a highly developed urban culture, with expertise in mining, farming, engineering, road building,

Italy has been ruled by emperors, popes, monarchs, and democratically elected presidents and prime ministers. The country has experienced periods of astonishing development, from the grandeur of the Roman Empire and the beauty of the Renaissance to devastating wars and the economic boom of the 1960s.

The Valley of the Temples in Agrigento, Sicily, forms part of the remains of an ancient city founded in the sixth century B.C.

sailing, painting, sculpting, and warfare. Etruscan women enjoyed equal status in society. They owned property, kept their names after marriage, and learned to read.

The Etruscans were also respected for their ability to predict the future. They read the entrails, especially the liver, of bulls, goats, and sheep for patterns that were seen as signs from the gods.

By about 800 B.C., the Greeks and Phoenicians had established colonies in the southern part of the Italian peninsula and Sicily, while the Etruscans dominated central Italy, especially the area between the Arno and Tiber rivers. A federation of tribes known as the Latin League flourished in the fertile region of Latium south of the Tiber. Rome was one of the most important states in Latium during the sixth century B.C.

THE ROMAN REPUBLIC

The first Roman republic was established in 509 B.C., with Rome as the capital. The city of Rome was built on seven hills: Capitoline, Palatine, Caelian, Esquiline, Aventine, Quirinal, and Viminal. The republic was governed by elected officials instead of monarchs, and the constitution distributed political power by making the leader of the republic answerable to the senate or legislature.

Roman society was divided into three classes—at the top of the social ladder were the patricians, members of the aristocracy; next came the plebeians, the common people; and at the bottom were the slaves. The male patricians and plebeians could fight in the army and participate in politics, but the slaves were not considered citizens of the republic and had no such rights.

THE FOUNDING OF ROME

Rome has a well-known legend that tells how the twin brothers Romulus and Remus founded the city. Their father was Mars, the god of war, and their mother was Rhea Silvia, daughter of the local king Numitor. Rhea's uncle, Amulius, had forcibly taken the throne. When the twin boys were born, Amulius seized them, put them into a basket, and threw them into the River Tiber. He hoped that they would drown, because he saw his niece's children as a possible threat to his kingship in the future. However, the boys were rescued by a she-wolf, who fed the babies with her own milk and cared for them. The boys were raised by a shepherd, Faustulus.

When they reached adulthood, they discovered who they were and killed Amulius (right). They decided to build a city of their own, but could not agree on the location—Remus favored the Aventine Hill, but Romulus wanted to use the Palatine Hill—so each built a separate city. One day Remus and Romulus had a fight over whose city was best, and Romulus killed his brother.

Romulus named the new city Rome, after himself. The legend says that Romulus populated his new city with runaway slaves and convicted criminals, becoming the first king of Rome in 753 B.C. Romulus went on to create the Roman Legions and the Roman Senate.

In the early years of the republic, many conflicts arose between the patricians and the plebeians over the latter's involvement in government. The plebeians finally forced the lawmakers to develop a written legal code called the Law of the Twelve Tables. Engraved on bronze tablets, which were displayed in the Roman Forum, this code had great significance for future democracies. It recognized that male patricians and plebeians had equal rights and dealt with such legal matters as writing contracts, property rights, debt, marriage, divorce, and criminal punishment.

An artist's impression of the Ides of March, where Julius Caesar was brutally stabbed to death.

EARLY CONQUESTS By 272 B.C. the Romans ruled the whole Italian peninsula, having defeated the Etruscans in the north and the Greeks in the south. During the third and second centuries B.C., Rome fought the north African city-state Carthage for domination of the western Mediterranean Sea in a formidable struggle called the Punic Wars. Famous Carthaginian commander Hannibal invaded Italy in 218 B.C., and using African war elephants, defeated Rome at the battles of Trebbia (218 B.C.) and Cannae (216 B.C.). Finally, in 146 B.C., the Romans destroyed Carthage. Victors in the Punic Wars, they secured the islands of Sicily, Sardinia, and Corsica, and parts of eastern Spain. Victories in the east gave them control of Greece. By 63 B.C. they ruled most of the Mediterranean.

JULIUS CAESAR Julius Caesar further expanded the republic by conquering Gaul (now France) in 51 B.C. Caesar was a military genius, talented orator, accomplished poet, and historian. Although he was a member of the aristocracy, he supported the plebeian cause. In 45 B.C. Caesar declared himself dictator of the Roman republic and ruler of its vast empire. Caesar believed in equality (he allowed all of Italy's male inhabitants to become Roman citizens), but he also believed that a dictator should have absolute supremacy and be able to choose his successor. Many Roman senators did not agree with him. On March 15 (called the Ides of March), 44 B.C. Julius Caesar was stabbed to death by a group of senators, including a man named Brutus, whom some believed to be Caesar's illegitimate son.

THE ROMAN EMPIRE

A decade of civil unrest followed Caesar's death, as Caesar's nephew, Julius Octavian, and Mark Antony struggled for power. In 31 B.C. Octavian became the first Roman emperor, taking the name Augustus ("the revered"). He

Life in the Roman Empire was filled with pleasures for the wealthy, who lived in large homes with up to 20 rooms, open central skylights, elaborate gardens, and walls decorated with beautiful frescoes. They lounged on couches in the dining room for their meals and visited public bathhouses to relax with friends and play dice. Slaves served food and beverages in the bathhouses and gave massages to customers and cleaned the baths.

Poorer Romans had small homes and found it hard to get jobs because the slaves did most of the hard work. But they did not starve, since all Roman citizens were entitled to free grain. Roman families often went to the temple to make offerings to the gods. Children were taught by Greek slaves at school, and in their spare time they played with small figurines, hoops, balls, and their pet cats and dogs. Boys wrestled and fenced as well.

The Romans fed their love of entertainment by going to the theater. Greek tragedies and comedies, ballet, and mime were popular performances. Audiences were allowed to shout their comments to the actors and dancers on stage.

The Romans also enjoyed watching gladiator fights, where slaves fought each other or wild animals to the death, and chariot races, where drivers had to stay on their chariots (right) or risk being dragged by the reins or trampled by the horses.

built libraries, temples, theaters, and roads, and established a uniform legal code in the empire. His rule began a time known as Pax Romana, or "Roman Peace." The empire reached its peak by the end of the first century A.D., with the Roman Empire stretching from the Caspian Sea in the east to the Atlantic Ocean in the west and from northern Britain in the north to Egypt in the south.

By the third century, the empire was in decline. Roman territories were repeatedly invaded by barbarians from eastern Europe and central Asia. In A.D. 285 Emperor Diocletian divided the empire into the Eastern Byzantine Empire, ruled from Constantinople (now Istanbul), and the Western Roman Empire, ruled from Rome. Christianity had become widespread throughout the Roman Empire during the centuries, and Emperor Constantine the Great legalized the religion in A.D. 313. The Western Empire later fell after invasions by the Visigoths and the Vandals from central Europe. The last Roman emperor was deposed in A.D. 476, ending the Western Empire.

THE MIDDLE AGES

The gothic Scaliger Tombs (Arche Scaligeri) at the church of Santa Maria Antica in Verona. This is a burial monument for members of the Scaligeri family.

From the end of the Western Roman Empire to the 16th century, Italy was invaded and occupied by numerous neighboring armies and forces competing for dominance of the Mediterranean region. In A.D. 800 the establishment of the Holy Roman Empire across Germany and central Europe brought central Italy officially under the control of Charlemagne (Charles the Great) and the Roman Catholic Church, cutting off the north of the peninsula from the south. By the 11th century the north was controlled by the Lombards, a Germanic people with origins in southern Sweden; the central region by the Catholic Church; and the south by Norman adventurers from northern France.

By the end of the 12th century much of Italy was divided into small city-states that had achieved some independence from their official rulers. The city-states had strong commercial ties with the rest of Europe and prospered. They were populated by successful merchants and skilled artisans. Many were run by rich and powerful families such as the Visconti of Milan, the Scaligeri of Verona, the Gonzaga of Mantua, and the Medici of Florence.

THE RENAISSANCE

The Italian Renaissance that began in the late 14th century was an era of great artistic and intellectual achievement. In the 15th and 16th centuries wealthy members of the merchant class contributed to the birth of a great cultural movement in Italy called the Renaissance, or "rebirth." Renaissance thought emphasized human beings as masters of their own destiny rather than as victims of fate, and rejected religious explanations of phenomena.

The ideal Renaissance person possessed a great deal of knowledge about many subjects, both scientific and artistic. Leonardo da Vinci, for example, was a highly accomplished artist, scientist, and engineer. The Renaissance thinker embraced classical Greek notions of beauty and art and lived according to an ideal where the human being as an individual could direct his or her life in a rational manner.

Cities, the Church, and leading Renaissance families supported the arts, commissioning painters, sculptors, architects, and poets for many projects. Italy thus accumulated a great wealth of art and cultural and philosophical knowledge that had an enormous impact on Western European thought and ideas for centuries afterward.

FOREIGN DOMINATION

The Italian city-states lost much of their autonomy in the 16th—18th centuries as the French and Spaniards fought over Italian territory during the Wars of Religion, Thirty Years' War (1618—48), and the War of the Spanish Succession (1701—14). After the latter half of the 16th century, the Spaniards dominated most of Italy. Only Venice and the duchy of Savoy-Piedmont retained some independence.

Austria became a major power in the north after the War of the Spanish Succession ended in 1713, while the Spanish Bourbons dominated the south and the popes retained their hold over the central states.

At the end of the 18th century a French republican army led by Napoleon Bonaparte invaded northern and central Italy. By 1799 Napoleon controlled much of Italy and took over its administration. He retrained the Italian army, revised the legal system, built bridges and schools, restored roads, ended the feudal system of land management, and took property away from the papacy. By instituting these reforms and inspiring nationalism among the Italian people, Napoleon gave Italy a sturdy foundation for independence.

INDEPENDENCE AND UNIFICATION

After Napoleon was defeated in the Battle of Waterloo in 1815, the victors restored Italy to its former monarchs: Lombardy and Venetia went to the Austrians, the papal states to the Pope, and Naples and Sicily to the Bourbons. Piedmont remained an independent Italian state under the rule of the king of Sardinia, Victor Emmanuel I.

In 1831 Giuseppe Mazzini, a revolutionary from Genoa, began the Risorgimento, or "Resurgence," a movement to unify all of Italy. Two other figures played key parts in the Risorgimento movement: King Victor Emmanuel II and his prime minister Camillo di Cavour (1810—61).

Cavour sought the help of France's Napoleon III after the Piedmontese army fought two losing battles against the Austrians in 1848 and 1849. In the War of Liberation in 1859, Italian and French forces defeated the Austrians and captured Milan and Lombardy.

An illustration of Count Camillo Benso di Cavour, the first prime minister of the new Kingdom of Italy.

In 1860 most of northern and central Italy voted for a unified Italian state, but the Pope did not favor unifying the papal states with the other regions. Giuseppe Garibaldi (1807—82), a freedom fighter and Mazzini's ally, united southern Italy and the island of Sicily with the north and later took the papal states as well. In March 1861 the united Kingdom of Italy was proclaimed, with Victor Emmanuel II as the first king of its 22 million citizens.

But two territories were still outside the rule of the new kingdom: Venetia (under Austrian rule) and Rome (under papal rule). In 1866 Venetia was ceded to Italy; in 1870 Rome was captured.

THE ITALIAN KINGDOM

Despite having a central government, the new Kingdom of Italy was unstable. Cavour died soon after unification, and there were no able leaders to take over the job of administering the different regions, each with its own distinct language and customs.

The first 35 years of the kingdom saw 33 different governments. The challenges facing the early leaders included widespread illiteracy and poverty. Between 1860 and 1920 millions of Italians emigrated, hoping to find a better life elsewhere. The leaders needed to find a way to unify provincial systems of law and taxation and raise national consciousness.

GIUSEPPE GARIBALDI

Born in 1807, Giuseppe Garibaldi was an Italian patriot and military leader who is generally considered the founding father of modern Italy, along with Giuseppe Mazzini and Victor Emmanuel II, king of Sardinia. Garibaldi was a key leader of the Italian Risorgimento (Resurgence), since he personally commanded and fought in many military campaigns that led to the creation of a unified Italy. He fought campaigns in both South America and Italy, earning him the title "Hero of Two Worlds." Garibaldi's most famous military exploit occurred in 1860, when he landed in Sicily at the head of a revolutionary force known as the Thousand Red Shirts. The great general defeated the opposing Neapolitan troops, conquered the island and later captured Naples. He was a skilled orator and leader, and gained admiration and support outside of Italy, especially in the United States. He remained a national hero in Italy until his death in 1882. Statues of Garibaldi can be seen in many Italian town and city squares today.

When World War I broke out in 1914, Italy allied itself with Austria and Germany. However, Italy chose not to participate when Austria waged war against Serbia. Italy broke away from Austria and Germany in 1915 and joined forces with the Allies, France, Great Britain, and Russia, in exchange for territory. Italy lost 600,000 people, killed during the war.

THE FASCIST ERA

In the aftermath of World War I, Benito Mussolini, a charismatic and ambitious politician, became leader of Italy. In 1921 Mussolini founded the Fascist Party and won 35 seats in the parliament. He was appointed prime minister in 1922 and became dictator in 1925. Mussolini outlawed all political parties except his own Fascist Party, dissolved trade unions, censored the press, had his enemies murdered, and created a secret police to deal with communist and socialist opposition. Under his authoritarian rule, the economy revived and order was brought to the country.

In 1936 Mussolini conquered Ethiopia. In 1939 Great Britain and France declared war on Germany. Italy joined forces with Germany in 1940 and became a key member of the Axis powers. Italian troops fought the British unsuccessfully in North Africa and were also involved in the Axis invasion of the Soviet Union in 1941. However, following the Allied invasion of Sicily in 1943, the king removed the increasingly unpopular Mussolini from office and signed an armistice with the Allies.

Germany later occupied Italy and reinstated Mussolini to rule in the north, although he had lost nearly every battle in France, Africa, Greece, and Albania. In 1944 Italy realigned against Germany, and in 1945 Italian partisans murdered Mussolini and his mistress.

THE ITALIAN REPUBLIC

Modern Italian politics has lacked stability since the end of World War II, with more than 60 different governments serving in that time. In 1946 Italians voted to make Italy a republic. The Christian Democrats won 35 percent of the seats in the new Constituent Assembly.

In 1947 Italy gave up Ethiopia, and a new constitution in 1948 reinstated the freedoms removed by the Fascists and established a parliamentary system. The economy revived in the 1950s, with financial assistance from the United States under the Marshall Plan. In 1957 Italy joined the European Economic Community (EEC) and enjoyed great economic growth.

Between 1974 and 1982 terrorist groups tried to bring about social change by murdering politicians (including Christian Democrat prime minister Aldo Moro in 1978), journalists, policemen, or anyone in authority. Many of these terrorists were sentenced to life in prison.

From 1983 to 1987 Bettino Craxi, the first Socialist prime minister, served the longest uninterrupted term since World War II. In 1992 a corruption scandal implicated politicians from almost all the parties. The coalition government, led by Giulio Andreotti, resigned and a caretaker government of nonpoliticians led the country to general elections.

In 1994 an alliance of political parties, led by Forza Italia, won a majority of seats, and media and sports tycoon Silvio Berlusconi took office as prime

Obsessed with his public image, *Il Duce* (or "The Leader") as Mussolini liked to call himself) would stand on a stool at official gatherings to look tall and strong.

minister. Romano Prodi, a center-left candidate, won the 1996 election, but was ousted from office in 1998. Italy joined the European Monetary Union (EMU) in 1999 and adopted the euro in 2002.

In 2001 Berlusconi was re-elected as prime minister, but lost the next election to Prodi in 2006. Berlusconi was returned to power in 2008, but left office in 2011 amid scandals about his private life, ending his 17-year domination of Italian politics. Mario Monti, an Italian economist, served as Italy's Prime Minister from 2011 to 2013. Italy's new Prime Minister, Enrico Letta, pledged to stimulate growth and jobs, while easing some of the unpopular austerity measures enacted to lower Italy's cumbersome debt.

An economist and academic, Mario Monti resigned from office in December 2012. Italy's next prime minister, Enrico Letta, took office on April 28, 2013.

INTERNET LINKS

www.bbc.co.uk/schools/primaryhistory/romans/

This educational BBC history website offers an overview of Roman history, culture, art, lifestyle, technology, and religion, with teacher resources and games.

www.bbc.co.uk/science/leonardo/

This excellent website provides a brief overview of Leonardo da Vinci and the Renaissance with links to the artist's ideas, art, and historical timeline.

www.learner.org/interactives/renaissance/

This site includes links on the Renaissance—a movement that revolutionized Europe and Italy—with links to important developments such as the printing press, the birth of exploration, new ways of thinking, and the development of science.

www.encyclopedia.com/topic/Giuseppe_Garibaldi.aspx

This site offers a detailed account of Giuseppe Garibaldi's life and achievements, with photographs and links to related topics.

GOVERNMENT

Originally a palace designed by Gian Lorenzo Bernini, the Palazzo Montecitorio in Rome is now the seat of the Italian Chamber of Deputies.

3

ITALY HAS BEEN A PARLIAMENTARY republic since June 2, 1946, when Italians voted to abolish the constitutional monarchy that had led the country since 1861 and institute democratic rule. The Italian republic is governed by the constitution of 1948, which guarantees freedom of speech, thought, and the press.

DIVISIONS OF GOVERNMENT

The Italian government is made up of the president of the republic, a bicameral parliament, a cabinet of ministers, and courts of justice.

The parliament has two chambers: the Senate of the Republic and the Chamber of Deputies. The Senate consists of 315 elected members. Seven senators are elected for life—they are either former presidents of Italy or people chosen by the president who have outstanding merits in social, scientific, or artistic fields. Six senators represent Italians living outside Italy. Senators must be more than 40 years old.

The Chamber of Deputies has 630 elected members who represent 32 electoral constituencies. Twelve deputies are elected by Italians living abroad. Parliament members serve five-year terms. The two chambers have equal powers, and all laws must be passed by both of these bodies.

The president of the republic is the head of state, elected by the parliament and 58 regional representatives to serve for seven years. The president must be at least 50 years old. He or she has the power to veto laws, but majorities in both parliament houses can override the presidential veto. The executive arm of the government is headed by

Like the U.S. Constitution, the Italian Constitution of 1948 guarantees certain fundamental rights for each person. It guarantees every citizen personal liberty, freedom of thought and information, freedom of association, and the right to own private property. The constitution also places on every citizen a duty to protect and uphold the laws of the country.

a president-appointed prime minister, who nominates the members of the cabinet, or Council of Ministers. The current president is Giorgio Napolitano, who was elected in May 2006.

The judicial arm consists of civil and criminal courts, administrative courts, and a constitutional court. Italy's judicial system is based on ancient Roman law. Judges dominate in court cases, serving as the "lawyers," who investigate the facts, question witnesses, and decide the verdict, and as the jurors. Juries attend only the most important cases.

LOCAL GOVERNMENT

Italy is divided into 20 regions: 15 with ordinary status, five with special autonomy. The ordinary regions are Abruzzi, Apulia, Basilicata, Calabria, Campania, Emilia-Romagna, Lazio, Liguria, Lombardy, Marche, Molise, Piedmont, Tuscany, Umbria, and Veneto. The special regions are Friuli-Venezia Giulia, Sicily, Sardinia, Valle d'Aosta, and Trentino-Alto Adige.

The president of the Italian Republic resides at the historical Quirinal Palace in Rome.

REGIONAL POLITICS

Regional identity remains a powerful force in Italian politics. Italy's autonomous regions reflect deep ethnic and regional differences in modern Italy. The process of Italian unification in the late 19th century, as well as the failure of Mussolini to promote a pan-ethnic Italian identity during the 1920s and 1930s, encouraged Italians to see their interests and affairs in regional terms. As a result many regional political parties exist across Italy that promote regional issues and seek greater regional autonomy. For historical reasons, the differences between Italian regions can be seen as a North-South divide.

Among the larger regional parties is the Lega Nord *(Northern League), which was founded in 1991 (right). They campaign for greater regional autonomy, especially for the north of Italy. They draw a lot of support in the regions of Veneto, Piedmont, and Lombardy, and promote northern Italian culture and ideas. Their focus is more on local identity as a unifying ideology, and they draw from both the left and right of the political spectrum. Howev er, controversial head of the separatist* Lega Nord, *Umberto Bossi, resigned on April 5, 2012 in the heat of a corruption scandal. The party treasurer, Belsito, is also being investigated for possible connections with the 'Ndrangheta, a powerful criminal organization based in Calabria in southern Italy.*

The south of Italy has followed a quite separate historical path for many centuries, reflecting the position and influence of the Kingdom of Sicily, which covered much of southern Italy and Sicily from the early 12th century until 1816. Following the end of World War II, the Sicilian Independence Movement fought for an independent Sicily until the early 1950s. More recently, the Movement for Autonomy party has campaigned for greater regional independence, although often as part of the ruling coalition, the center-right People of Freedom coalition. The Sardinian Action Party also campaigns for greater autonomy in Sardinia, but its support and influence have fallen away in recent years.

A politcal rally for the Communist Refoundation Party at the Piazza della Repubblica in Rome.

Each region is governed by a council that can pass laws specific to that region. The council elects the president and members of the executive committee. The regions became autonomous so that local culture and language could be taken into account, and their councils generally have more freedom than those of the ordinary regions to make legislative decisions. Another reason why limited autonomy has been granted to these regions is so that it will be less likely they will seek independence.

The regions are further divided into provinces. Italy has 110 provinces, each governed by an executive council and a governor. The provincial government is responsible for social services and the construction and maintenance of roads among other things.

Italy has about 8,100 communes—towns, cities, and metropolitan centers—run by municipal councils. The communal governments are responsible for urban planning, health, municipal public works, public transportation, and education.

INDEPENDENT STATES

Italy has two independent states within its borders: Vatican City and the Republic of San Marino. Vatican City, located in Rome, was created in 1929. The Lateran Concordat signed by Cardinal Pietro Gasparri and Benito Mussolini on behalf of Pope Pius XI and King Victor Emmanuel III, respectively, restored the Catholic Church's political power and exclusive rights to the Vatican since Italy took the papal states in 1870. Vatican City comes under the protection of the Italian police.

With a population of just 32,000, the tiny Republic of San Marino has an independent government made up of three branches: executive, legislative, and judicial. San Marino has its own constitution and currency and maintains diplomatic relations with other countries.

"Everything is not political, but politics is interested in everything."
— Niccolò Machiavelli, 16th-century Italian historian and philosopher.

POLITICAL PARTIES

Italians believe strongly in democracy, and many still fear a takeover by extremist parties. This is why, historically, there have been so many parties in parliament. Italian elections are dominated by multiparty alliances. Party power is all-encompassing in Italy. A system of patronage hands out government jobs according to political affiliation. One's job, house, promotion, and pension may depend on the secretary or other official of the local party. If the Christian Democrats run your district, it makes sense to join their party, take part in their social events, and make sure that they stay in power—even if they are incompetent.

COALITION GOVERNMENTS

The Italian way of government is not as volatile as it may seem. The Christian Democrats dominated the country's coalition governments from the end of World War II (in 1945) to the mid-1990s. However, in the 1990s, when the "Clean Hands" investigation uncovered a corruption network involving many political parties, the Christian Democrats was split into factions.

In the 1994 election, the Socialists won a small number of seats. Forza Italia, a new right-wing, pro-free market party, also gained steady support. In 2001 the center-right House of Freedom coalition won the majority in both the Senate and Chamber of Deputies, followed by the center-left Olive Tree coalition. Led by Silvio Berlusconi, the House of Freedom included the popular Forza Italia, which held key government posts from 2001—2006. The two new groupings greatly simplified Italy's previously diverse range of parties, and left no space for the historically powerful Communist party.

Berlusconi's House of Freedom coalition lost the 2006 election to Romano Prodi's eight-party, center-left Union coalition. However, a snap election was called in 2008 after the government lost a key vote in the Senate. Silvio Berlusconi's new right-wing coalition, People of Freedom—which combined Forza Italia with the National Alliance—won 344 seats in this election, ousting the sitting government. 2013 saw a new political partnership when the center-left Democratic Party and the People of Liberty, a center-right group, united behind new prime minister Enrico Letta.

"We owe it to our children to give them a dignified and hopeful future."
— Italian President Giorgio Napolitano

THE MAFIA—ITALY'S OTHER "GOVERNMENT"

Since the 19th century the southern regions of Sicily, Calabria, and Campania have been controlled to a large extent by the mafia. Originally established to maintain order in the lawless regions of Sicily, the mafia resolved conflicts in the community because there was no effective government. But the mafia method was often cruel, using intimidation and violent means to achieve results. Members, known as mafiosos, were sworn to a code of silence that prevented them from testifying against fellow members.

After Italy was unified, the mafia helped politicians win votes in exchange for favors. Southern Italians looked to the mafia to protect them and even paid it taxes. Many saw the mafia as a positive force in the community. Although Mussolini tried to wipe out the mafia by forcing its members to leave the country, many returned after World War II.

In the late 1970s and early 1980s the Italian government made a brave decision to halt mafia activities. Spurred by the murders of anti-mafia officials and their families, the government made it a crime to be a member of a mafia organization. In 1987, 14 mafiosos broke the code of silence to provide incriminating evidence against hundreds of their brothers. Some 338 mafiosos were convicted in the largest mafia trial in Italian history.

The murder of two judges in 1992 caused a strong reaction in Italy. In 1993 senior boss Salvatore "Totò" Riina was arrested; his successor, Leoluca Bagarella, was arrested in 1995. Anti-mafia efforts continued through the rest of the 1990s, resulting in the arrest of more bosses. In 2002 some 300 mafiosos in high-security jails began a hunger strike to protest against the tough conditions of their incarceration—cell isolation, one visit and one phone call a month, and two hours of outdoor exercise a day—especially as lawmakers discussed proposals to extend the length of the prison term under such conditions.

The mafia has inspired books, films, television drama series, and even video games: Mario Puzo's best-selling novel, The Godfather, *which was adapted by Francis Ford Coppola into the 1972 Oscar award—winning movie by the same title; the television series* The Sopranos, *which won four Golden Globe awards in 2000; and the controversial video game* Mafia: The City of Lost Heaven.

ATTITUDES TOWARD GOVERNMENT

The Italian government and civil service are known for being inefficient. Long lines are normal at banks and social service agencies. Applications for government services take years to be reviewed, and government intervention does not often solve problems. Criminal cases can take years to come to trial. Italians rarely pay attention to new laws passed by the government.

Somehow this inefficiency does not seem to bother Italians. Many have either grown to tolerate bureaucratic red tape or have found ways to get around it.

Italians often rely on relatives or close family friends to get things done. Many have little respect for the institution of government. They do not trust government officials, and some do not pay their income taxes.

Even so, Italians follow political events with a passion. Italian politics is rarely boring and directly impacts their lives.

INTERNET LINKS

www.indexmundi.com/italy/government_profile.html

This website shows the profile of the Italian government.

http://globaledge.msu.edu/countries/italy/government/

This website provides information on Italian politics and foreign relations.

www.italylogue.com/regions-of-italy

This site provides a map and an introduction to all of the regions in Italy.

www.independent.co.uk/news/uk/crime/unstoppable-spread-of-calabrias-ndrangheta-mafia-sees-outposts-established-in-uk-and-ireland-7876558.html

This news article is about the spreading influence of an Italian mafia crime cartel in Europe.

ECONOMY

The Banca d'Italia (Bank of Italy) in Rome is the central bank of Italy and part of the European System of Central Banks and the Eurosystem. Its main role is banking and financial supervision to protect the stability and efficiency of Italy's financial system.

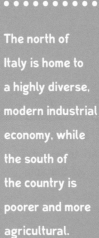

4

T HE CONTRAST BETWEEN THE rich and the poor in Italy is very noticeable. A wealthy northern Italian might shop on Milan's fanciest streets, dressed more fashionably than a wealthy Parisian, while a farm laborer in the underdeveloped south works 10-hour days just to make ends meet.

Before World War II, many Italians lived no better than laborers in one of Europe's poorest countries. The postwar years saw the transformation

The north of Italy is home to a highly diverse, modern industrial economy, while the south of the country is poorer and more agricultural.

Vineyards in Serralunga d'Alba, Piedmont. Agriculture, especially vineyards, is still an important part of the industrialized Italian economy.

A salt lake in Cagliari, the capital of Sardinia.

of Italy from a largely agricultural nation to one of the major industrial powers of Europe. This was a period of strong economic and industrial growth now commonly referred to as the Boom.

Between 1945 and 1960, Italy's industrial output expanded by a staggering 150 percent. Industries in the north grew substantially, and many southerners moved up north to take factory jobs. Advanced farm machinery replaced human labor and changed the country's economy from a primarily agricultural one to an industrial one. Income levels doubled, and people began saving and investing their money.

By the 1960s unemployment in Italy was almost negligible. By the 1970s Italy ranked among the world's top seven industrial powers. As economic growth continued into the 1980s, at a slower but still reasonable rate of 3 percent per year, Italy briefly displaced Great Britain as the fifth-largest industrial power in the world, following the United States, Japan, Germany, and France. In 2012 Italy was the world's seventh-largest economy.

The Italian economy slowed in the 1990s to an average annual growth rate of 1—2 percent annually, before picking up again in the new millennium, with a more than 2.5 percent annual growth rate. However, following the financial crisis and depression of 2008—12, Italy's economy has shrunk by almost 7 percent.

Italians are Europe's biggest savers, saving an average of 21 percent of their income. With their industrial and economic talents, Italians have been called Europe's most adaptable and innovative entrepreneurs.

TRADE AND EMPLOYMENT

Italy's primary natural resources include natural gas and crude oil, fish, coal, and land for farming. The country trades internationally in minerals and metals, textiles and clothing, vehicles, and food products.

Italy's main trading partners are Germany, France, the Netherlands, Spain, and the United States. About 6 percent of Italian exports go to the United States, and 5 percent of Italy's imports come from the United States. But the bulk of Italy's trade occurs within the European Union (EU), of which Italy is a member. About 60 percent of Italy's imports come from EU countries, which buy about 57 percent of Italian exports.

Most of the 25 million working Italians are employed in one of three sectors: agricultural, industrial, or services. The service sector employs 65.1 percent of the labor force, industry 30.7 percent, and agricultural production 4.2 percent.

Italy's unemployment rate was 11.6 percent in 2013, with youth unemployment at 36 percent. Stimulating industry and employment, especially in the agricultural south where an average of 20 percent of the labor force is jobless, is a central concern for the government. Parliament has passed a labor market reform bill aimed at making the labor market more inclusive and flexible. This bill promotes open-ended and apprenticeship

Cranes at the trading port in Genoa.

contracts for young workers, makes unemployment insurance more universal, and encourages hiring.

AGRICULTURE

There are more than 2.6 million farms in Italy. Italy's agricultural products include wheat, corn, soybeans, tomatoes, potatoes, sugar beets, citrus fruit, grapes, and olives. Italy is the world's largest producer of wine and olive oil. Olives are grown mainly in the southern regions of Apulia and Calabria, while wine is produced in every region. Although Italy cultivates a large amount of wheat, it still imports substantial amounts, mostly from its EU trading partners.

Farms occupy about 25 percent of Italy's total land area. Most farms are small—about 7 acres (3 hectares)—and family owned. Only 5.2 percent of the labor force is employed in agriculture today, compared with more than 50 percent before World War II.

The traditional method of hand-picking olives and letting them fall into nets for collection is still practiced in many parts of Italy.

MINING AND ENERGY

Italy is one of Europe's poorest countries in mineral resources. It has natural reserves of iron ore, feldspar, quartz, sulfur, coal, mercury, and zinc, but imports other minerals.

Most of Italy's natural gas supply is imported; the rest is produced in the Po River Valley. The government is working to reduce the nation's use of crude oil in favor of coal and natural gas.

A 1987 referendum rejected the use of nuclear power in Italy, and construction of nuclear power plants was abandoned. But Italy may have to rethink its non-nuclear policy in order to meet its energy needs; more than 75 percent of its energy is imported.

INDUSTRY

Italy's heavy industry is concentrated in the Milan—Turin—Genoa triangle in the north. Major industrial products include steel, iron, computers, motor vehicles, chemicals, and textiles. Italy also has a large petroleum refining industry.

A window-making factory in Lombardy.

Italian industry is driven by a few large corporations and many small-and medium-sized enterprises. Three top Italian companies are Olivetti (IT and telecommunications), Fiat (automobiles), and Pirelli (tires). Small enterprises are considered the backbone of Italy's economy. The country has more small family establishments than do other European countries. Italians like to keep their businesses small so that the family can maintain control.

Businesses in the same industry tend to gather in one location. For example, Italian silk manufacturers are located in Como and ceramic makers in Sassulo.

FASHION

Italian fashion has brought great distinction to the country. Italian designers are known for their bold and innovative experiments with color and form.

Milan is the fashion capital of Italy. The city is home to some of the world's most important design labels: trendy clothing for young people by Luciano Benetton; exquisite men's and women's wear by Giorgio Armani; Krizia knits by Mariuccia Mandelli; elegant clothing in unusual fabrics by Miuccia Prada; Missoni sweaters by Ottavio and Rosita; Gucci "classic" clothing and accessories; and shoes by Ferragamo, the company that preserves founder Salvatore's "art of the shoe." Every October fashion editors and buyers from around the world gather in Milan to view the season's collections.

Founded in 1899 in Turin, Fiat (named from the acronym for Fabbrica Italiana Automobili Torino) is Italy's largest and most famous automobile manufacturer and Italy's largest industrial group.

In 2009, Fiat and the U.S. carmaker Chrysler formed an alliance which, in 2011, led to Fiat taking a majority interest in Chrysler. Fiat-Chrysler is an international auto group that designs, produces and sells vehicles for the mass market under the Fiat, Lancia, Alfa Romeo, Fiat Professional and Abarth brands, as well as luxury and performance cars under the Ferrari and Maserati brands. Jeep and Chrysler are other brand models that the Group produces in North America and are distributed in Europe through Lancia-Chrysler and Jeep sales networks. Fiat also operates in the components sector, through Magneti Marelli and Teksid, and in the production systems sector through Comau.

Fiat-Chrysler sold a combined total of more than 4 million vehicles for the year 2011, making it the seventh largest automaker globally. The Group owns companies located in 44 countries and has customers in approximately 140 countries.

In 2013, a full merger of the two companies is being worked out. If successful, this will make Fiat the world's third-largest automobile group after Toyota and Volkswagen.

The Ferrari Museum was opened on founder Enzo Ferrari's birthday — February 18, 1990, one and a half years after he passed away. It receives about 240,000 visitors a year.

One of Italy's most important fashion designers was Gianni Versace. Born in 1946 in Calabria, he moved to Milan in 1972 and was part of the first wave of designers who put the city on the fashion map. In 1989 he began to design haute couture, or high fashion, and soon became famous for his innovations in women's wear. With his sister and brother-in-law, he created a multimillion-dollar empire. Tragically, he was shot outside his home in Miami in 1997. His family continues to run the Versace fashion empire.

SERVICES

Almost two-thirds of the Italian labor force is employed in the service sector, including tourism, an important sector of the economy, with 43 million tourist arrivals in 2010, making it the fifth most visited country in the world.

A worker at an orange processing and packing factory in Sicily.

THE ITALIAN WORKDAY

Italians maintain a healthy balance between work and leisure. Work is often a family affair, and a lot of time off is also spent with the family. Italians generally do not spend as much time at work as many North Americans do. Stores in Italy usually close for a few hours in the middle of the day and stay open into the evening. Only restaurants stay open in the middle of the day.

In general most businesses in the north operate from 9:00 A.M. to 5:00 P.M., with a one-hour lunch break. In the central and southern regions, businesses operate from 9:00 A.M. to 1:00 P.M. and 3:00 P.M. to 7:00 P.M. Banks and government offices are usually open only from 8:30 A.M. to 1:30 P.M.

Italians generally work five-day, 40-hour weeks. They have 10 paid public holidays and six weeks of paid vacation. Historically many workers receive a bonus of one month's salary in December and a cost-of-living increase every quarter. However, since the economic downturn of recent years, pay and conditions have been less generous.

ECONOMIC PROBLEMS

Workers going on strike in Milan.

Italy's two main economic problems, since its impressive postwar record, are its large budget deficit and wide income disparities.

Italy's budget deficit is due, in large part, to widespread tax evasion. Many Italians from different walks of life, from professionals, small businesspeople, laborers, even to the rich and famous, do not pay taxes on additional income. Experts estimate that if people's earnings in this submerged economy were accounted for, Italy's gross domestic product (GDP) figure would be about 20 percent greater.

Its budget deficit was a major barrier to Italy's entry to the European Monetary Union (EMU), which regulated currency and economic policy. At 6.5 percent in 1996, the deficit was far greater than the 3 percent maximum to qualify for membership. Italy underwent political and economic reform to get into shape. The government sold public industries and cut wage protection and social security to try to balance the budget.

When the euro was launched in 1999, Italy's budget deficit had fallen to 2 percent, less than the 3 percent requirement. Although the country failed to meet another EMU entry criterion (its national debt exceeded 60 percent of the GDP), Italy still made it into the club of nations sharing the euro. In 2002 Italy sustained a budget deficit of 1 percent of the GDP.

Wide wealth gaps exist between the economically disadvantaged South—which has been compared to a Third World or underdeveloped country—and the industrialized North. The poorest regions in Italy are Calabria and Campania. The South records a high unemployment rate of 20 percent, a situation compounded by higher illiteracy and birth rates than in the North.

As a result income levels are considerably lower in the South. The per capita income in Palermo in Sicily is only half that of Turin in the northern region of Piedmont. Industrial development in the South is also far behind that in the progressive North. Although the government offers incentives to industries to relocate in the South, many major corporations hesitate to do so because of mafia activity in much of the region. The economy in the South has thus remained largely agricultural and pastoral.

A train station in Italy. With unemployment on the rise, many younger Italians move from city to city in search of better employment opportunities.

More recently the Eurozone crisis has hit the Italian economy hard. In 2011 the Italian public debt stood at 120 percent of gross domestic product (GDP)—roughly double the level that is considered safe. In 2012 the Italian government's credit rating was downgraded by international banks because the country was seen as a higher credit risk. Former Finance Minister Mario Monti was appointed Prime Minister after the resignation of Silvio Berlusconi in late 2011 precisely to steer Italy through the difficult economic times. In late 2012, Monti announced his resignation. After weeks of political deadlock and an inconclusive general election, Enrico Letta became Italy's new prime minister, taking office on April 28, 2013.

INTERNET LINKS

www.italianculture.net/english/fashion.html

This is a guide to Italian fashion since 1950, with photographs and links.

www.italia.it/en/home.html

This official Italian tourism website provides photographs, video, and other links to Italian regions, culture, news, and sites.

ENVIRONMENT

The village of Castelluccio in Umbria as seen from the Great Plain in Monti Sibillini National Park. The park offers one of the most spectacular displays of wild flowers in the world.

5

ENVIRONMENTAL PROTECTION in Italy was practiced as far back as ancient Roman times. The scholar known as Pliny the Elder (A.D. 23—79), in his study of life titled *Pliny's Natural History in Thirty-Seven Books*, described how the Romans managed their natural resources, with systems for administering forests and planting trees, classifying plants and detailing their special properties, and classifying protected forests.

Italy has established several governmental agencies to confront its environmental problems, including the Ministry for Ecology and the Ministry of Culture and Environmental Quality.

The stunning Gschnagenhardt-Alm and Geisler mountain range found in Trentino-Alto Adige/Südtirol, an autonomous region in Italy.

The town of Vernazza sits by the rugged coastline of Cinque Terre. It is part of the Cinque Terre National Park and is a UNESCO World Heritage Site.

The first wildlife reserves were set up in the 19th century as hunting areas for royalty, and the first national park was set aside in 1922.

Today, faced with the challenges of developing industry to create employment opportunities, Italians have returned to their heritage of environmental consciousness, although some Italians have also received criticism for being slow to deal with the country's environmental issues, particularly air pollution, which has reached dangerous levels in some cities in the north. Membership in regional and international government organizations such as the European Union (EU) is also a strong motivation for Italy to preserve its natural environment.

PROTECTING NATURE'S GIFTS

Blessed with fertile volcanic soil, Italians have enjoyed the fruits of the earth for centuries. Over time, however, human settlement has greatly altered much of the country's natural landscape. Due to systematic logging in the 19th century, only 34 percent of the country is forested (according to 2005 estimates), while 26 percent of the land is arable. Denuded mountain slopes suffer from erosion and landslides.

Italians have been making efforts to protect what remains of their country's virgin forests since the early 20th century, and in 1988 the government formulated the first comprehensive forestry policy. One key proposal is to convert abandoned farmland to forest.

The main threats to Italy's wildlife are habitat loss and sport hunting, which have wiped out a significant proportion of the original wildlife, leaving the surviving species in protected areas. Italy has few large mammals: small populations of wolves, bears, and lynx in remote mountain areas and larger numbers of ibex, chamois, and red deer in the national parks. Hawks are common, but eagles are a rare sight.

Pollution in the Mediterranean Sea is a threat to Italy's marine life, including the monk seal, fin whale, and dogfish shark, which are now threatened or endangered species. Human activity on beaches, where turtles lay their eggs, reduces these gentle reptiles' chances of survival.

Italy has taken measures to clean up its inland waterways and help reduce the human impact on the Mediterranean Sea. The country's many national parks and other national and regional reserves and protected areas are refuges for surviving flora and fauna.

Volunteers, such as these boys in Milan, ensure that pollution in the forests is kept at bay.

FIGHTING AIR POLLUTION

Italy's biggest environmental problem is air pollution. The country ranks among the top five in the world with the highest number of cars owned per person. Fumes from factories and vehicles damage historic buildings and harm people's health. In 2002, when a two-month dry spell triggered a smog emergency in Milan (which lies under a chronic smog cloud in the Po Valley) and other cities in the northern Lombardy region, authorities advised people to avoid jogging or taking their babies out in strollers. In 2011 the capital city of Milan banned all vehicles for a day to fight the growing air pollution. About 120,000 vehicles were affected by this extreme action.

Italy passed a Clean Air Act in 1966. In an attempt to reduce industrial carbon emissions, Italy has turned to natural gas, a cleaner fuel alternative

ABRUZZO AND THE LYNX

The Abruzzo National Park (below), near the town of Pescasseroli, just a two-hour drive from Rome, was established in 1923. The main section of the park covers about 155 square miles (401 square km), but there are reserves surrounding it that bring the total protected area of Abruzzo to about 235 square miles (609 square km). Hardwood forests cover two-thirds of this area; beech, oak, ash, maple, and wild oak are found here. Some of the animals that live in the Abruzzo National Park are Marsican brown bears, chamois, mountain goats, foxes, and Apennine wolves. Many of these animals have been hunted to extinction outside the park.

In 1972 a cryptozoologist (a scientist who specializes in finding rare and endangered animals), Franco Tassi, shocked the biological community in Italy by suggesting that the Abruzzo National Park might still contain the lynx, a wildcat with short legs and a short tail. The lynx was long believed to have disappeared from the Italian landscape in ancient times. As manager of Abruzzo, Tassi and his team began to look for evidence of the lynx's existence. In 1995 they did a census, estimating that there were some eight to ten lynxes in the park, and the same year two pairs of lynxes mated. This was a happy story for Italy's wildlife; it is not often that animals once thought to be extinct are rediscovered in their natural habitat. Tassi thinks that the lynx may be on the rebound in the central and southern Apennines.

than coal. Italy set up an environment ministry in 1986, now called the Italian Ministry for the Environment, Land, and Sea. In the 1990s, Italy began to implement policy changes in line with its obligations as an EU member state.

EU member states are bound by the Kyoto Protocol, which represents the world's response to the thinning of the ozone layer caused by carbon gases. At the 1997 meeting in Kyoto, Japan, involving 160 countries, developed nations agreed to reduce their carbon emissions by 8 percent from 1990 levels between the years 2008 and 2012. Italy's antipollution measures, such as taxing oil more heavily than natural gas and installing electric-powered modes of transportation, are part of its efforts to fulfill its environmental responsibilities within the EU and the global community. However, Italy, together with Japan and Spain, constitute the three countries that are most failing to meet the targets set under the Kyoto agreement and are facing heavy penalties for this.

The government and "green" organizations are not the only ones involved in the fight against pollution. The Fiat Corporation has shown how corporations can do their part; Fiat signed an agreement to reduce emissions from its vehicles by 23 percent by 2010. Today Fiat has achieved its aims and set a new record by already reaching the European average goal of carbon dioxide emissions of 7.4 ounces/miles (130 grams/km) established for 2015.

The sleek Pendolino electric train, built by Fiat, tilts at curves to travel faster even on winding tracks. Today, the Pendolino runs in Spain, Germany, Finland, Switzerland, and Portugal.

CREATIVE SOLUTIONS

Italians have come up with some wonderful ideas for reducing their dependence on conventional, environmentally unfriendly technologies, such as gas-powered cars and coal-fired energy plants.

CAR-SHARING In 1999 Italy pilot-tested an electric car-sharing program in nine major cities, including Milan, Rome, Turin, Florence, and Bologna. Each city received some 500 to 600 cars, which were made available in parking areas around the city for members of the program to use. People joined the program by paying a membership fee. They then received a special card with which to start an electric car and paid according to how far they traveled. The Italian government continues to invest millions in the car-sharing program.

CAR-FREE DAY In February 2000, 174 Italian cities participated in the nation's first "no-car Sunday." To encourage car owners to leave their vehicles at home that day, public transportation was made free in many cities. Museums also waived their entrance fees to encourage people to spend the day enjoying the exhibits.

Italy's car-free day has since been repeated every first Sunday of the month from February to May every year. Pollution levels in Turin have fallen

An electric-powered smart car charging its batteries at a street station in Rome. Given its small size, the smart car is perfect for Italy's narrow streets.

by as much as 56 percent on "no-car Sundays."
Going car-free in the long run, however, means
more than leaving the car at home for a few
hours on one day of the month; it means a
lifestyle change, a committed decision on the
part of car owners to give up their cars and
switch to bicycles or rented electric cars.

SOLAR POWER The 10,000 Photovoltaic
Roofs program is the Italian government's
five-year plan to equip 10,000 buildings
nationwide with rooftop solar panels for
electricity generation starting from 1998. The
government, in their National Action Plan
for the Renewable Energy Sources, is now
focused on its 2020 target to increase the use
of solar photovoltaic power further, in line with the European Union's climate
and energy objective of having 17 percent of the country's primary energy
stemming from renewable sources.

The bicycle sharing program, such as this one in Milan, is another creative solution for commuters to get around without the use of environmentally unfriendly technologies.

INTERNET LINKS

www.ultimateitaly.com/national-parks/

This website is dedicated to providing detailed information on all of
Italy's national parks.

www.minambiente.it/home

This is the official website of the Italian Ministry of the Environment,
Land, and Sea, which is responsible for environmental issues.

www.lifeinitaly.com/life/noise-in-italy.asp

This website offers a personal view on living with noise pollution in Italy.

ITALIANS

Sardinians in their traditional costumes preparing for the La Sartiglia Carnival in Sardinia. La Sartiglia is a sort of medieval tournament with knights wearing fabulous costumes and white androgynous masks.

6

W ITH A POPULATION of more than 61.4 million, Italy is one of the most crowded nations in Europe. The average nationwide population density is 512 inhabitants per square mile (198 per square km). However, the distribution is uneven. Most Italians live in large cities and on the coasts and plains.

Lombardy, Campania, and Lazio are the most densely populated regions, with populations of 10 million, 5.8 million, and 5.7 million, respectively. Many other areas are still underpopulated. Valle d'Aosta, Basilicata, and Sardinia are the least densely populated regions, with populations of 130,000, 611,000, and 1.68 million, respectively.

Urban Italians account for more than two-thirds of the population. Rural Italians made up about half the population before World War II, but many have moved to the urban areas. Rome is the most populous city, with more than 3.4 million inhabitants. Milan, Naples, and Turin follow, with populations of 3 million, 2.3 million, and 1.7 million, respectively. Palermo and Genoa are home to between 855,000 and 872,000 people each, and Bologna and Florence to around 370,000 each.

Despite being predominantly Roman Catholic, Italy has one of the lowest birth rates in the world, as Italians choose to have small families. Women living in the northern regions tend to have fewer children than the 1.4 national average, while women in the southern regions tend to have more. The infant mortality rate of 3.36 deaths per 1,000 births is lower in the north than in the south.

A traditional Italian family sitting outside their home in Pozzuolo, Umbria.

There are approximately 9 births, 10 deaths, and 4.7 migrants for every 1,000 of the population. A longer average lifespan due to improved health care and a low rate of population growth have resulted in an aging society. More than 20 percent of Italians are 65 years old or older, compared with approximately 14 percent under age 15. The median age stands at 43.5 years.

ETHNIC GROUPS

Italians in the North differ from their southern counterparts not just in lifestyle and wealth, but also in physical appearance. Northern Italians generally look similar to German and French people, whose ancestors conquered northern Italy in past centuries. Southern Italians, taking after their ancient Greek colonizers, have a distinctly Mediterranean look, with a darker skin tone, dark hair, and brown eyes.

Several minority groups live in Italy's different regions: French-speakers in the Valle d'Aosta region along the French and Swiss borders; German-speakers around the city of Bolzano in the Trentino-Alto Adige / Südtirol region along the Austrian and Swiss borders; Slovene-speakers in Friuli-Venezia Giulia; and Albanians in small communities in the southern regions.

Immigrants from Ethiopia, Egypt, and the Philippines also live and work in Italian cities such as Rome. They generally congregate in certain sectors of the city and establish their own neighborhoods and stores. The bigger cities also attract Gypsy families, mostly from eastern Europe, but their numbers are difficult to calculate. The population of foreign residents in Italy was estimated at more than 4.5 million as of January 2011.

MIGRATION

One factor that has profoundly affected Italy's population patterns is migration, both within and across the country's borders. Since the mid-1800s millions of Italians have resettled in other parts of the world. Between 1850 and 1880 more than 100,000 Italians left the country annually, many from the south. They headed first for France and Switzerland and later for North and South America.

German folk dancers wearing their traditional German-Austrian attire in Rome. German-Italians account for about a quarter of Italy's population.

By 1910 more than 6 million Italians had settled in the United States. The U.S. Immigration Department then implemented a literacy test for immigrants. In 1921 a quota system was imposed, limiting the number of Europeans migrating to the United States. In 1924 the newly enacted National Origins Act further restricted entry into the United States, especially for immigrants from southern and eastern Europe.

Italian emigration picked up again after World War II. Between 1946 and 1973, 8 million Italians left their country and settled in Germany, France, and Switzerland.

Not until 1973 did Italy's massive international migration patterns reverse, as more Italians returned home and fewer left the country. Emigration continued to ease in the 1980s, and immigration intensified. Since the 1980s Italy has been undergoing high levels of immigration after many decades of net emigration.

In 1999 at least 50 percent of Italy's immigrants came from Albania, China, Morocco, Romania, and the Ukraine.

Internal migration often takes the form of rural-urban migration. In the 1950s and 1960s many Italians moved from the south and northeast to Rome and the growing Milan-Turin-Genoa industrial area in search of employment and a better quality of life.

REGIONALISM

Many Italians identify more strongly with their region than with their nation. It is not unusual to meet Italians who insist that they are Tuscan or Venetian or Piedmontese, not just Italian.

People from different regions and cities are associated with certain personality traits. For example Piedmontese are perceived to be prouder and more reserved than people from other regions; Milanese are said to be more business-minded and sophisticated; Neapolitans are known to be easygoing; Romans are perceived to be aggressive and Venetians passive; and Florentines love to try new things but continue to revere their Renaissance past.

If there is any animosity among Italians from different parts of the country, it is strongest between the urban North and rural South. The South, below the imaginary Ancona Wall stretching from the Adriatic port of Ancona to southern Rome, is also referred to as the Mezzogiorno, which means "Land of the Midday Sun." The South occupies about 40 percent of Italian land and is home to around 32 percent of the population, but contributes only 20 percent of the GDP.

Many Northerners, particularly those living in the country's most important industrial cities, regard the primarily agricultural and pastoral south as being backward. Since World War II the Italian government has spent billions of dollars to raise the standard of living in the south, but the economic and social gap between the two regions continues to widen. Northern Italians resent the government's focus on the South and what they consider a misuse of taxpayers' money. They feel that the money goes straight into the corrupt hands of criminal organizations such as the mafia, whose influence is still strong in the South. Southern Italians, on the other hand, feel that the North has long meddled in their affairs without making much progress.

A Sardinian farmer with his donkey. Many prosperous and progressive Northerners feel superior to their poorer Southern compatriots.

CLASS DISTINCTIONS

Although Italy does have a class system, there is more mobility between classes than in other Western European nations. Some social scientists divide Italy's social system into the elite or governing class, the middle class, the urban proletariat, and the rural class. The elite class (about 10 percent of the population) is made up of the nation's intellectuals and professionals and wealthy businesspeople and landowners. The middle class (about 35 percent of the population) is made up of educated people with defined job skills, such as white-collar workers, artisans, and small businessmen. The urban proletariat (about 35 percent of the population) consists of the less educated but stable working class. The rural class (about 20 percent of the population) consists of small landowners, tenants of landowners, and day laborers. Some hold additional part-time jobs, while others are migrant farmers who travel from region to region, finding work where they can.

A driver standing by his truck. Social status used to be determined by wealth, family history, and family connections. Today, it is increasingly being measured by merit and education.

INTERNET LINKS

http://library.thinkquest.org/20619/Italian.html

This website provides information about migration patterns of the people of Italy to America throughout history.

www.nationmaster.com/country/it-italy/peo-people

This website from Nationmaster includes detailed statistics on all aspects of the Italian population, including divorce and marriage rates and age structures.

www.greatitalians.com/

This website lists the names of famous Italians from every industry throughout history.

LIFESTYLE

Milanese enjoying their leisure time at Galleria Vittorio Emanuele II, a luxury shopping mall and an architectural masterpiece. The Galleria was built in a Neo-Classical style from 1865 to 1877.

7

ONE THING VISITORS to Italy notice right away is the people's openness and sociable nature. Whether they live in a palazzo or a small apartment, Italians have a love of life and enjoy life's pleasures to the fullest.

Looking good is important, and many Italians have a natural flair for style. Italians are also known for their love of art and they encourage creativity in their own children.

A few seeming contradictions mark Italian culture. Although Italians admire cosmopolitanism, for example, they also respect tradition. They dislike authority, yet accept government inefficiency with little complaint. Italians are highly individualistic but they respect the institution of the family and, generally, make dutiful sons and daughters and responsible mothers and fathers.

Unlike in many North American cities where commercial activities are segregated from residential areas, in Italy, stores, offices, houses, and apartments mingle together seamlessly. Downtown areas are still alive and bustling in the evenings, when stores and offices have closed. Most buildings have storefronts facing the street and apartments facing the interior courtyard. Almost every block has restaurants and cafés, so the streets maintain a buzzing social atmosphere nearly every hour of the day and night.

APARTMENT LIVING

Most Italians live in cities, where multistoried apartments are the dominant form of housing, since they make the best use of limited

Italians enjoy socializing in bars, restaurants, and pizzerias, but gatherings at home are also very much a part of social and family life in Italy.

Colorful apartment houses in Burano, Venice. Apartment living is a way of life in most Italian cities.

urban space. A typical modern apartment occupies around 1,000 square feet (93 square m). Large cities such as Milan, Rome, and Naples face the problem of providing adequate, affordable housing for the lower and middle classes. The poor often live in small, two-room dwellings or in shanties on the outskirts of the city. In Rome rents are high, and new apartments come without closets, light fixtures, and kitchen appliances. In older buildings, plumbing can be unreliable and elevators may not always work or users may have to insert a coin before the door opens. Electricity can be expensive, and so central heating is only used when necessary.

VILLAS

Italian villas, or country houses, are usually made of brick or stone, with a tiled roof, and have two levels and an enclosed courtyard. Villas built in the 17th century can still be seen in the rural and suburban areas. They have two or more levels, several courtyards, and elaborate columns.

A group of 16th-century villas near Venice attracts art historians and tourists every year. The villas, including the Villa Trissino and Villa Capra, were the works of Andrea Palladio (1508—80), the most influential Italian Renaissance architect. Palladio invented a new style of housing—the country house—to meet both the practical and aesthetic needs of noble families living in the countryside. The Palladian style later spread to northern European countries such as England.

Old villas in Italy's big cities may look a little rundown on the outside but are often magnificent on the inside, with windows framing views of quiet and peaceful courtyards. Many old villas have been restored and redecorated, with marble floors, high ceilings, and antiques or modern Italian-designed furniture. These serve as holiday homes for the wealthy or as inns for tourists.

"(Italians) judge men and events less by what they read or learn, and far more by what they see, hear, touch, and smell."
—Luigi Barzini, in
The Italians

The larger villas may have a swimming pool in the courtyard, lovely gardens, separate annexes, and many rooms.

Many upper-class Italian families own villas in the countryside where they go to spend their weekends or holidays. Some of these estates have been passed down for generations; others are old farmhouses that have been renovated for modern living. In the countryside the lower floor of the villa may be used to store farm equipment; in the city it may function as a shop, garage, or office. The family usually lives on the second floor, while guest bedrooms fill the higher floors.

The famous Villa Capra, or Villa Rotunda, designed by Andrea Palladio. It is an Italian Renaissance villa located just outside the town of Vicenza. It is completely symmetrical with a central circular hall.

NATURAL ELEGANCE

Italians are known to be very conscious of their physical appearance and the image that they project to others. Projecting an image of refinement and culture known as *la bella figura* (lah BEL-lah fe-GOO-rah) is important to Italians of all social classes, from both the cosmopolitan north and the underdeveloped south. Italians show *la bella figura* in many ways: they behave considerately; they bring flowers or gifts to thank their host for dinner; they give and receive favors and compliments gracefully.

Many urban Italians dress well for work. They wear stylish Italian-made clothes to the office: an exquisitely cut suit with a silk tie for men; a soft skirt and blouse and fine leather heels for women.

Italians almost never wear shorts when going to a large city. They wear jeans, but their casual attire is often of high quality. When going to the opera, men wear suits and ties and women wear evening dresses. Black-tie attire is appropriate for opening nights at the famous opera houses.

Italians love wine, but they rarely drink themselves to the extent of being drunk, as most do not like to appear slovenly and out of control.

La bella figura shows even in towns and villages, especially on major feast days when visitors join the festivities.

Italians appear to
be resigned
to the fact that
their country does
not run as
smoothly as some
other European
nations do.

INSTITUTIONAL INEFFICIENCY

Although Italians pay attention to individual competence, they have had to put up with incompetence on the part of institutions and bureaucracies. The postal service, transportation system, telephone company, hospitals, schools, and government offices are notorious for being inefficiently managed and chaotic.

Domestic mail can take at least seven days to reach the addressee. Local checks take six days to clear, and foreign ones take 15 days. Trains and buses rarely run on time, and the major cities have appalling traffic jams and pollution problems.

The telephone system is confusing, with four-, five-, six-, seven-, and eight-digit phone numbers. Only half of all calls get through with the first dial. Installing a new phone can take up to a year. Mobile phones have become extremely popular, with Italy projected to have 100 million mobile subscriber connections in 2016 with Vodafone taking 30 percent of the market share. Despite an increase in the number of state and private hospitals, especially in the central and southern regions, the health care system still faces the problems of rising costs and bureaucracy. Schools follow rigid administrative rules, and staff at government offices face stacks of unprocessed forms.

Even the legal system is affected. Italy is said to be the land of 250,000 laws. Acts passed in ancient times are still in use today, along with the modern legislation. Laws are often modified several times before reaching the statute book.

Most Italians have grown accustomed to institutional inefficiency in their country. They pay more attention to personal relationships instead and are governed by social institutions such as family and the Church. Government rules and regulations are not nearly as effective in keeping chaos at bay as is a son's duty to his mother or a sinner's to God.

IMPORTANCE OF THE FAMILY

Italians may not be wholeheartedly loyal to government or nation, but they are truly devoted to family. The individual matters a lot, but not at the expense of the family. Italians believe that the family name is all-important and should not be tarnished by the thoughtless acts of one family member.

Pride in the family and the desire to keep family ties and values strong have probably been responsible for keeping the country together and enabling it to prosper in spite of its economic, social, and political problems.

Italians spend more time together as a family than do people from many other Western cultures. The traditional Italian family is based on the patriarchal institution—it is headed by the grandfather, who passes his authority on to the eldest son, who does the same to his first son, and so on through the generations. Children usually live with their parents until they get married. Then they join the family business, set up house near their parents, eat with them, visit them, and travel with them. More aged parents live with their children in Italy than in the United States, and many Italians feel that it is their duty to care for their parents themselves rather than place them in a nursing home. The grandparents help make important domestic decisions and often take care of the children when the parents go to work.

An Italian family getting together for a meal. Many married Italians try to set up house near to their parents.

In the northern, highly industrialized areas of Italy, the influence of the traditional family has dwindled as society has become wealthier and the cost of living has risen. Many Italians living in expensive, crowded cities, such as Rome and Milan, can only afford small apartments without extra rooms for their parents. Many of Rome's elderly now live on their own, with no family to care for or depend on them and without money to live in private homes for the aged.

Even the nuclear family is getting smaller. More Italian women today have jobs outside the home, either for financial independence or to supplement the family income. This often leads to the decision to have fewer babies. Northern Italy registers a significantly lower birth rate than southern Italy, and the national population growth rate ranks among the lowest in Western Europe.

CHILDHOOD HAS ITS PRIVILEGES

Italian families may be shrinking in size, but parents remain devoted to their children. Italians are generally very affectionate toward children. Parents readily hug and kiss their children in public and will even reach out to touch strangers' children whom they think are beautiful.

Children are regarded as equal members of the household in Italy—they are allowed to express their opinions and are treated as individuals with their own personalities. Italian children are very comfortable with their parents and readily admit (when they are grown up) that they truly love their parents.

Italian parents are ambitious and self-sacrificing for their children without being pushy. They are not likely to encourage their children to learn to read or to play an instrument at a young age. They feel that children will develop these skills in good time if so inclined and should not feel pressure to achieve before they are ready.

Parents also want their children to have what they did not have themselves when they were young. They hold elaborate parties to celebrate their children's birthdays and First Holy Communion Day, inviting many guests who arrive with gifts for the child.

ITALIAN MASCULINITY

Italian men pay courteous attention to women, opening doors for them and paying for dinner at restaurants. Traditionally, Italian men headed their families and saw themselves as protectors of the women in the household, upholding the honor of their wives, daughters, and mothers. However, the emergence of the nuclear family has gradually altered the balance of power between men and women in the household.

ITALIAN FEMININITY

Italian women are great nurturers, the main source of warmth and affection in the family. They provide the meals for the family, a very important task especially in a food-worshiping culture. They make sure that the children are properly fed and clothed and that they learn good manners and the difference between right and wrong.

Until the 1960s Italian mothers were not encouraged to work outside the home; their lives were focused on looking after the family. Many women were illiterate, because their families did not think it necessary to send them to school.

A group of children with their school bags heading to class.

The 1970s saw a feminist revolution in Italy, as women aggressively pursued equal rights with men under the law. In 1970 divorce was legalized in Italy, despite opposition from the Vatican, and women were assured the right to receive alimony and child support from their former husbands. Abortion was legalized in the late 1970s, a drastic step for a country dominated by Roman Catholics. Italian women can even get government funds to have an abortion.

Italian women gained equal rights in the workplace in 1977. The law ensured that women were paid the same as men in similar jobs. Today working women in Italy are entitled to five months of paid (at 80 percent of their salaries) maternity leave, usually taken two months before delivery and three months after. They are entitled to another six months of paid (at 30 percent of their salaries) parental leave, taken before the child turns three years of age. Mothers are also guaranteed the right to return to their jobs before the child reaches his or her first birthday.

Before World War II few Italian women were employed outside the home or farm. As in many Western nations, most women in Italy today work to help support the family. Italy has a significant proportion of women lawyers, doctors, professors, business managers, and parliament members. About 25 percent of Italy's doctors are women, and 40 percent of the Fiat labor force is made up of women.

Certain likes and dislikes and do's and don'ts offer glimpses of the Italian character:

Italians are expressive. They tend to gesticulate when talking, especially when bargaining for lower prices in small stores and open markets. Young couples freely display their affection in public.

Football, or soccer, is a national obsession, and Italians are passionate supporters of their favorite clubs. Cycling and basketball are also national sports, but baseball has not caught on.

Italians express themselves most beautifully in the arts; their painting, sculpture, and music have won admirers worldwide.

Italians love food. They take wine and olive oil very seriously; both are basic ingredients in Italian cooking. Extra virgin olive oil also adds flavor to salads, breads, and soups. Alcoholic beverages are served day and night at bars and restaurants (there is no official age limit for buying and drinking alcohol). Getting their first taste of wine at a young age among family, Italians learn to appreciate wine and drink in moderation.

Italians "live on the edge." Many are habitual cigarette smokers, although cigars and pipes are generally not popular.

Motorists drive fast and aggressively, changing lanes abruptly and going through red lights at a whim. Small cars squeeze into any available parking space—even on sidewalks.

EDUCATION

Education is compulsory and free for Italian children aged 6 to 14 years. Private schools under the Ministry of Education follow a curriculum similar to that used in public schools.

Mothers who work outside the home may send their toddlers to nursery school or their 5-year olds to kindergarten. Children aged 6 through 10 must attend *scuola elementare* (sko-OH-lah eh-leh-men-TAH-reh), or elementary school. Elementary schoolchildren take subjects such as Italian, mathematics, history, and science. Many elementary schools follow a half-day program six days a week. From ages 11 to 14 years, all children attend *scuola media* (MEH-dee-ah), or middle school. They study the same subjects as in elementary school in more depth and also take up a second language.

After 14 years of age, Italian children can discontinue their education or go on to *liceo* (LEE-sjeh-oh), a five-year upper-secondary school where they can specialize in vocational training or prepare for a university education. Subjects in the vocational program include agriculture, business, and aeronautics. Subjects in the pre-university program include literature, science, Latin, Greek, philosophy, fine arts, and history. Most middle- and upper-class children choose the path toward university.

Italian students have to study diligently to cope with difficult school examinations that are held regularly. Secondary school students have to pass a two-day oral and written examination in order to graduate and qualify for admission to university.

Established in 1088, the University of Bologna is the oldest institution of higher learning in all of Europe. Many Italian universities are overcrowded today. Most programs take four years to complete, while degrees in architecture and medicine take five and six years, respectively.

INTERNET LINKS

http://library.thinkquest.org/CR0212302/italy.html

This website provides an article written from a child's point of view on family and general life in Italy.

www.lifeinitaly.com/lifestyle

This site contains information about the culture and way of life in Italy, including clichés and Italian humor.

www.understandingitaly.com/profile-content/education.html

This website provides information about the education system in Italy, including the different types of schools available.

RELIGION

A fish-eye view of the ornate interior of Saint Peter's Basilica in Vatican City. With Michelangelo on its design team, the Basilica Papale di San Pietro in Vaticano was built in a late Renaissance style and is one of the largest and most famous churches in the world.

8

T HE ANCIENT ROMANS worshiped many gods and incorporated them into a lunar calendar of 355 days. The Romans showed their devotion by building temples dedicated to the gods. Worshipers left offerings of milk, wine, money, jewels, and statues at temple altars and held elaborate public ceremonies and sacrificed animals to win favor from the gods on family matters and for good fortune.

Roman cults led by different groups of priests worshiped one or more gods and followed strict rules.

Priests from all over the world coming together to attend a Mass held at Saint Peter's Basilica.

The Gothic Milan Cathedral, or Duomo di Milano, is the largest cathedral in the world by area—216,800 sq feet (20,139 m²).

Christianity was born in the first century A.D. among the followers of Jesus of Nazareth. As the religion spread, Roman rulers, especially the Emperor Nero, began persecuting Christians. Of all religions that existed in ancient Rome, Christianity was the least tolerated and was banned everywhere in the Roman Empire. However, Christianity continued to attract converts until it became the official religion of the empire in the fourth century, when the Emperor Constantine saw a vision of a cross in the sky and became a devoted Christian.

From the fall of the Roman Empire to the unification of Italy's many city-states in 1870, Roman Catholicism was the strongest force holding the people together. The popes who ruled the Catholic Church had tremendous influence, both spiritual and political, over Italy for centuries. In 1929 Roman Catholicism was made the state religion of Italy. Religious instruction in state schools was mandatory, and the Church had the legal right to censor films, books, and stage plays if they went against Catholic doctrine or portrayed the Church in an unfavorable light.

In 1984 the Church and the state formally severed ties in an official concordat, although the document reaffirmed the Church's importance in the moral lives of Italians. The Vatican, located within the city of Rome, is a separate sovereign state. It is also the home of the Pope and the center of the worldwide Roman Catholic Church.

THE ANCIENT ROMAN GODS

The ancient Romans worshiped a main pantheon of six gods—Apollo, Jupiter, Mars, Mercury, Neptune, and Vulcan—and six goddesses—Ceres, Diana, Juno, Minerva, Venus, and Vesta—led by the Capitoline triad of Jupiter—Juno—Minerva. Most of the Roman gods were in fact Greek gods with Latin names. The Romans admired Greek civilization and adopted many of its elements.

The Romans also adopted gods from other cultures, such as Isis from the Egyptian pantheon and Cybele, the Turkish goddess of motherhood. The Capitoline triad was adopted from the Etruscans, who also honored a main pantheon of 12 gods, although the Roman gods are more identified with the Greek gods.

Each god was responsible for a different aspect of the universe. Jupiter, king of the gods, was god of the sky. Juno was the goddess of women, Mercury the god of merchants, Vulcan the god of fire, Mars the god of war, Minerva the goddess of wisdom, and Venus the goddess of fertility and love. After the establishment of the Roman Empire, emperors were also worshiped as gods after their death.

The central niche of the famous Trevi Fountain in Rome features a statue of Neptune.

RELIGION AND LAW

Roman Catholicism was Italy's strongest unifying force throughout its turbulent history, but since the country's post-World War II economic boom, urbanization and growing prosperity have reduced the influence of religion on the country's politics and laws.

Saint Mark's Basilica in Venice is one of Italy's best-known examples of Byzantine architecture and a symbol of early Venetian wealth and power.

Over the last few decades the Italian people have decided that they prefer to make their own decisions rather than follow the rules of the Church. In the 1970s laws were passed legalizing abortion and divorce, both still forbidden by the Roman Catholic Church. Birth control is widely practiced, although the Church also forbids it. In a 2006 survey 83 percent of Italians favor abortion if the mother's life is in danger.

More than three-fourths of the population do not think that the Church should have anything to do with the country's political system. Catholics have traditionally supported the Christian Democratic Party.

ROMAN CATHOLICISM AND ITALIAN SOCIAL LIFE

Twenty-six percent of Italians who participated in a Gallup poll in 2007–2008 responded that religion is unimportant in their lives.

Church attendance has fallen dramatically. Although in smaller towns some people might be motivated to go to church, just so the neighbors will not talk, in the cities, parishes are so big that people do not notice who attends church and who does not. Changing lifestyles have also affected church attendance. Rural Italians traditionally associate the fertility of the land with devotion to God and the Church but, with fewer people working the land, the significance of religion from this perspective has diminished.

Although official surveys show that approximately 30 percent of Italians attend Mass every Sunday, a study by the Patriarchate of Venice in 2007 found that figures were lower and only 23 percent actually go to a church regularly.

Regular churchgoers in Italy today are generally children, women, the elderly, and rural folk, particularly in the South. Many men who attend church are farmers, technicians, craftsmen, and clerks. Members of the upper and lower classes do not attend Sunday Mass as often as do members of the middle class.

However, these statistics do not tell the whole story. Although most Italians are not regular churchgoers, many of them place more faith and trust in the Church than they do in the government. Moreover, a great majority still turn to the Church for the important rites of passage in their lives: more than 90 percent are baptized in church and make their first Holy Communion; around 80 percent are confirmed; and nearly all have church weddings. Even members of the Italian Communist Party, which does not encourage religious ties, often participate in these rites.

Most important the Church sets a moral example for the people. Whether or not modern-day Italians strictly follow the teachings of the Church, the Church helps people to be aware of the difference between right and wrong and of the importance of showing compassion to those in need.

The Church's primary responsibility in Italy today is to help people who are in trouble. The Church provides health and welfare services to the needy; implements programs for prostitutes, the elderly, and drug addicts; and runs homes for the disabled. It also provides employment aid for people who are out of work, food and shelter for the hungry, and of course religious education for children.

The Roman Catholic Church is a tremendous source of pride for the average Italian. The Vatican in Rome is an immensely important institution, the capital of the Roman Catholic world and residence of the Pope (the successor of the first leader of the Church, the Apostle Peter). Vatican City contains some of the world's finest art and architecture, including Saint Peter's Basilica, one of the country's architectural masterpieces, which attracts millions of visitors every year.

"... whether he goes to church or not, Catholicism is still part of the Italian's psyche in the same way as lungs or a kidney are part of his body. ..."
—*Italian Labyrinth: Italy in the 1980s* by John Haycraft.

VATICAN CITY

Saint Peter's Square (Piazza San Pietro) in the walled enclave of the Vatican City, Rome. The Vatican City is the smallest independent state in the world by area and population.

Vatican City was granted sovereignty and independence from the Holy See in 1929 by the Lateran Treaty between Prime Minister Mussolini and Pope Pius XI. Although Vatican City occupies less than 0.17 square miles (0.44 square km), it is a fully functioning miniature state.

The largest and most important structure in Vatican City is Saint Peter's Basilica, the world's largest church. The Vatican's colorfully dressed Swiss Guards, trained in martial arts and the use of light weapons for the protection of the Pope, make up the world's smallest army.

There are almost 2 million volumes in the Vatican library as well as thousands of Latin, Greek, Arabic, and Hebrew manuscripts, and about 6,000 volumes are added every year. Vatican Radio broadcasts to global audiences in 40 languages, and the Vatican also has its own newspaper, stamps, and prison. Many Nobel Prize winners are members of the Vatican's prestigious Pontifical Academy of Sciences.

The Vatican is famous for its stunning art treasures: sculptures of the saints by 17th-century artist Gian Lorenzo Bernini atop the giant "arms" encircling the piazza of Saint Peter's Basilica; Michelangelo's magnificent *Pietà* sculpture, the Roman sculpture *Apollo Belvedere*, and Raphael's fresco *The Liberation of Saint Peter* in the museums; and Michelangelo's famous frescoes, which took four years to paint, covering the 10,000-square-foot (900-square-m) ceiling of the Sistine Chapel.

The Pope grants a general audience every Wednesday in the piazza of Saint Peter's Basilica. When Catholics see him, they shout "Viva il Papa!" (VEE-vah eel PAH-pah), or "Long live the Pope!" When meeting the Pope in person, worshipers call him either "Santissimo Padre" (sahn-TEE-see-moh PAH-dray), which means "Holy Father," or "Sua Santità" (SWAH sahn-TEE-tah), which means "Your Holiness."

The current Pope, elected on March 13, 2013, is Francis. There have been 266 former popes. The Pope's official title is Bishop of Rome, Vicar of Jesus Christ, Successor of the Prince of the Apostles, Supreme Pontiff of the Universal Church, Patriarch of the West, Primate of Italy, Archbishop and Metropolitan of the Roman Province, Sovereign of the State of Vatican City, and Servant of the Servants of God.

Catholics, aged 16 to 35 years old, have a chance to meet the Pope at the week-long World Youth Day conference, held every two years in a different city. Millions of young people, including non-Catholics, have gathered in Rome, Denver, Buenos Aires, Manila, Paris, Toronto, and other cities since Pope John Paul II started the event in 1984.

Some 1,000 people, consisting of cardinals, church officials, altar boys, students, and Swiss Guardsmen, are permanent residents of the Vatican. The most important is the former Cardinal Jorge Bergoglio, or Pope Francis. He is known for his less formal, "no frills" approachable style—on the night of his election, he took the bus back to his hotel with the cardinals rather than be driven in the papal car.

OTHER RELIGIONS AND FOLK BELIEFS

About 10 percent of Italians follow other religions. Many of Italy's Protestants belong to the Waldensian Church, started by Peter Waldo in the 12th century

According to ancient Roman legend, Rome was founded in 753 B.C. by Romulus, who was abandoned with his twin brother Remus near the Tiber River in Rome when they were babies.

The twins' mother was the virgin princess Rhea Silvia, who had been raped by Mars, the god of war. The babies were saved by a female wolf—who allowed them to suckle her for milk—and brought up by a shepherd. When Romulus grew up, he decided to build a city on the spot where he had been saved. According to ancient Roman writings, Romulus marked out the four corners of the city, plowed a ditch from corner to corner to delineate the city boundaries, and built a wall to fortify the area.

In 1990 Italian archaeologist Andrea Carandini set out to prove that the myth of Rome's founding was based on truth. By digging 20 feet (6 m) under the Palatine, one of the seven hills of Rome, Carandini uncovered the wall he believed to be the one erected by Romulus. Nearby he found pottery dating back to about 730 B.C., further evidence that Rome was founded during the time of Romulus. In fact Rome is believed to be named after Romulus. The statue showing the baby brothers suckling from a she-wolf dates back to Etruscan times. Unfortunately Carandini had to discontinue his search due to lack of financial support.

in southern France and northern Italy as a reaction against the Roman Catholic Church.

Jews make up the other significant non-Catholic group in Italy. Some are descended from families who lived in Rome as far back as the pre-Christian era, others came from Spain in the 15th century, and still others came from

Germany and Poland in the late 19th and early 20th centuries. Most of the Jewish community is centered in Milan and Rome, while Florence and Trieste have small congregations. An old Jewish neighborhood—synagogues and kosher restaurant intact—still survives in Rome.

Muslims, mostly students and immigrants from North Africa, make up another significant religious group in Italy. Other minority groups include the Buddhists and many Italians, particularly in the southern regions, still maintain folk beliefs. Some women in small villages are said to have magical powers. They are consulted for potions or charms to win the hearts of lovers, for predictions about the future, or for lottery numbers. Some Southerners fear witches and actually perform animal sacrifices to keep them away.

Inside a synagogue in Casale Monferrato. Jews in Italy are well assimilated into the local population.

INTERNET LINKS

www.nationmaster.com/country/it-italy/rel-religion

This website provides detailed statistics on various religions practiced in Italy.

www.catholic-hierarchy.org/country/it.html

The website contains information on the Catholic Church in Italy, including details about hierarchy, bishops, dioceses, and events.

www.euro-islam.info/country-profiles/italy/

This site provides key issues, news coverage, and analysis on Islam in Europe and North America.

LANGUAGE

Italians enjoy a quiet afternoon chatting with friends or catching up on the local news.

9

Currently 13 percent of the population of the European Union speaks Italian as a first language and 3 percent speaks it as a second language.

TALIAN IS A ROMANCE LANGUAGE descended from the Vulgar Latin dialect spoken by people living in the last years of the Roman Empire. Italian uses more Latin words than do other Romance languages such as Spanish and French, and it has a similar grammatical structure to that of Latin.

Latin is still the language of Vatican City in Rome; official papal documents are printed in Latin as well as seven other languages.

Italian is one of the most melodic and expressive languages in the world. Although Italians use their language eloquently and dramatically, they do not demand that foreigners speak it as well as they do. Italian

A Latin sign in Italy. Currently classified as a dead language, Latin originated in the Italian peninsula and was spoken in ancient Rome.

Young girls reading a book and other forms of media in modern Italy.

is spoken by more than 65 million people in Italy, Switzerland, the United States, Canada, Argentina, and Brazil.

OFFICIAL AND STANDARD ITALIAN

Official Italian used in business and the mass media is the dialect of Tuscany (Florence, to be precise), recognized throughout Italy as the purest dialect and most cultured accent. However, standard Italian leans more toward the dialect of Rome.

The Tuscan dialect became influential in the late 13th and early 14th centuries when Florence was at its political and cultural peak. Tuscan authors such as Dante, Giovanni Boccaccio, and Francesco Petrarca began to use their dialect in literary works.

Between the Renaissance and the mid-20th century, most Italians still spoke regional dialects. Only the educated upper classes both wrote and spoke "pure" Italian. Regional dialects caused communication problems among soldiers from different regions during World War I.

After World War II the Tuscan dialect became more standardized and was taught in schools. The literacy rate rose, and people became familiar with official Italian through emerging communication media.

REGIONAL DIALECTS

Other than the Tuscan and Roman dialects, many more regional dialects are spoken in Italy, such as Venetian, Aostan, Ligurian, Napoletano, Milanese, Corsican, and Occitan in the Piedmontese provinces of Cuneo and Turin. On the island of Sardinia alone, there are four different dialects, and there are also several Sicilian dialects.

Speaking a dialect is not the same as speaking with an accent. A dialect is a language variety with its own grammar and vocabulary. In Italy,

ITALIAN SAYINGS AND THEIR ENGLISH EQUIVALENTS

Some of the ideas behind common English sayings and proverbs are also expressed in Italian using different words:

Italian: You're speaking Turkish.

English: It's Greek to me.

Italian: When the cat is out, the mice are dancing.

English: When the cat's away, the mice will play.

Italian: Better an egg today than a chicken tomorrow.

English: A bird in the hand is worth two in the bush.

Italian: Much smoke but a small roast.

English: Much ado about nothing.

Italian: Drop by drop the sea is filled.

English: Little drops of water make the mighty ocean.

some dialects are so drastically dissimilar that two people speaking two different dialects may not be able to understand each other. In contrast people from different regions in the United States or England may speak with different accents and still be able to understand one another.

Many young Italians speak a dialect at home to their parents and grandparents, but converse in standard Italian when outside the home. Dialect is still the primary means of communication in small agricultural towns or villages and on small islands.

One reason why Italian dialects are so varied is that political unity is a recent reality in the country. Another reason is the geography of the landscape, isolating one region from another and allowing each dialect to flourish on its own. Many Italian dialects have been influenced by the languages of neighboring countries or of invaders who laid claim to the land at some point in the country's history.

Although most Italian dialects have Latin roots, the Aostan dialect is said to sound more like French, Venetian is sprinkled with Spanish and Portuguese words, and Piedmontese has a good deal of German. Southern Italian dialects have a Greek influence. Fortunately most dialects when written can be understood by any Italian speaker.

THE INFLUENCE OF ITALIAN AND VICE VERSA

During the Renaissance and the following centuries, Italy had an important influence on the cultures of France and England. Many Italian words made their way into the everyday speech of the French and the English, and many of these words have become so common in modern usage that few people recognize their Italian roots.

Numerous words that relate to music come from Italian: *libretto*, *maestro*, *mandolin*, *piano*, *soprano*, and *tempo*. Food words include *broccoli*, *cappuccino*, *espresso*, *minestrone*, and *salami*. Military terms, such as *battalion*, *cavalry*, and *colonel*, have been adapted from Italian.

Italian words used in English with the same spelling include *fiasco*, *fresco*, *ghetto*, *incognito*, *motto*, *solo*, *studio*, and *trio*. And then of course there is *ciao* (CHAOW), the word Italians use to say both "hello" and "good-bye," which has been readily adopted by many other cultures. Words such as *balcony*, *cartoon*, *sonnet*, and *zany* originate in 16th-century Italian. Other English words borrowed or adapted from Italian include *arcade*, *regatta*, *umbrella*, and *vendetta*.

In the opposite direction, English words have also found their way into Italian, especially since World War II. Some examples are *supermarket*, or *supermercato* (soo-per-mer-KAH-toh) in Italian, *popcorn*, *shopping*, *TV*, *poster*, *weekend*, *party*, *jeans*, and *cameraman*.

Dialects are still spoken by older Italians but are falling out of use amongst the young.

BODY LANGUAGE

Spoken Italian is said to be extremely expressive and persuasive. The dramatic gestures that Italians are famous for give the verbal language a new dimension.

HAND PURSE Probably the most characteristic Italian gesture (and the one most used by actors playing Italians), the hand purse consists of the fingers and thumb pointing upward, tips meeting to form a pocket or purse. To Italians, the hand purse indicates a question, such as "What are you doing?", "What do you want?", or "What do you mean?" In a tense situation, such as a traffic jam in Rome, an irritated Italian might lean out of his car window and hand purse forward to ask the person in the car in front of him, "What is going on?"

Locals dressed as Julius Caesar and a gladiator use the traditional thumbs up gesture as a nod to their ancient Roman heritage.

THUMBS UP This gesture was used by ancient Roman emperors in the Colosseum to indicate that a gladiator who had fought hard but lost should not be killed. (Thumbs down meant that the gladiator had to die.) Centuries later the thumbs up was reintroduced to Italians as an "okay" sign by American soldiers in World War II. Another American gesture meaning "okay," a ring made with the thumb and forefinger, means "zero" or "the pits" to northern Italians. To southern Italians, it is a major insult.

HANDSHAKE This is the standard greeting gesture for acquaintances. The average Italian who runs into someone he or she knows on the street will stop, shake hands, and chat, even if in a hurry, then shake hands again before moving on.

CHEEK SCREW Another typically Italian gesture, the cheek screw consists of the tip of the forefinger pressing into the cheek and making a screwing motion. This gesture is mainly used to indicate praise or to imply that something is especially good or beautiful. It is often used to compliment a good meal.

OTHER GESTURES Like almost everything in Italy, gestures have different interpretations in different regions. To a Neapolitan, pulling your eyelid is a warning to be alert; elsewhere in Italy, it might mean that someone is sly or cunning. In Rome and Naples, tapping the side of your nose is a friendly warning, while in Sardinia it indicates a shared secret. To flick your chin with your hand is a strong dismissive gesture meaning "I couldn't care less." In the South, however, it is interpreted as a simple, emotionless "no."

PERSONAL SPACE Italians have few inhibitions about personal space and standing close to one another. They are rarely self-conscious about embracing, and it is not unusual to see two men kissing each other on both cheeks. For both men and women, walking *a braccetto* (ah-bra-CHET-toh), or arm-in-arm, simply shows friendship. Many younger Italians stand up to show respect when an older family member or friend walks into the room.

Relatives and close friends often exchange hugs and kisses when greeting.

TITLES

Signore and *Signora* are the Italian equivalents of "Mr." and "Madam" or "Mrs." It is considered impolite in Italy to call an older person or a mere acquaintance by his or her first name until a firmer relationship has been established.

It is proper to show deference and respect for an engineer, doctor, lawyer, or professor by addressing him or her by the appropriate professional title: *Ingegnere* (en-jeh-NYEH-reh), *Dottore* (doh-TOH-reh), *Avvocato* (ah-voh-KAH-toh), and *Professore* (pro-feh-SOH-reh), respectively. *Don* and *Donna* are used before the first name of a person who has made an outstanding achievement or for whom one wants to show great respect.

OTHER LANGUAGES AND DIALECTS

Although Tuscan is taught in all the schools and is the official Italian language, some 5 percent of the population still use their own dialects.

Italian newspapers use the dialect of Tuscany.

People of German heritage living in Trentino-Alto Adige, or South Tyrol, speak German, as well as Italian. Other inhabitants of South Tyrol also speak Ladin, an ancient language similar to Romansh, one of the four national languages of Switzerland. In Valle d'Aosta, the majority of the inhabitants speak Franco-Provençal, followed by French, Walser (a Greman dialect), Spanish, and Portuguese. Some 50,000 people living in Piedmont also speak Provençal, a French dialect. Catalan, which is similar to Provençal, has been spoken in Sardinia since the 14th century.

Greek dialects are spoken in parts of Apulia. In Friuli-Venezia Giulia, which borders Slovenia and Austria, some ethnic groups speak Croat, Slovene, and German. Some communities in Calabria and Sicily speak Albanian. A small community of Armenians on the island of San Lazzaro in Venice speaks their own language. Gypsies in the North use the Sinthi dialect, while those in central and southern Italy use the Rom dialect.

INTERNET LINKS

www.italianlanguageguide.com

This website provides information about many aspects of the Italian language, including grammar, pronunciation, vocabulary, and history.

www.lifeinitaly.com/italian/language-history.asp

This site contains a short history of the Italian language, including its origins, its evolution, and its dialects.

www.evolpub.com/Italiandialects/ITALdial.html

This site provides information about the main dialects spoken in Italy, including some background and their characteristics.

In the 1930s and 1940s, Mussolini's Fascist regime tried to force ethnic groups into a national culture by eliminating foreign words from Italian. This campaign also included inventing new words to replace English ones. Donald Duck turned into *Paperino*, Mickey Mouse became *Topolino*, and Goofy was *Pippo*. In soccer, *goal* became *meta*.

ARTS

Shimmering Greek-Byzantine mosaics cover the interior of the
12th-century Palatine Chapel in Palermo, Sicily.

10

ITALY HAS INSPIRED THE WORLD for centuries with its remarkable artistic accomplishments. The ancient Romans were skilled engineers who built impressive monuments throughout their far-reaching empire. Italy was the birthplace of the Renaissance, the era that marked the transition from the medieval to the modern and produced a great revival in architecture, sculpture, painting, and literature.

In March 2012 art researchers in Florence claimed they may have found traces of an undiscovered Leonardo da Vinci work believed to be painted in 1504, concealed under a fresco.

The 17-foot (5.17-m) statue of *David* is a masterpiece of Renaissance sculpture created by Michelangelo between 1501 and 1504.

Leonardo da Vinci's famous 15th-century mural painting—*The Last Supper*—still stands in the convent and Dominican church of Santa Maria delle Grazie in Milan.

The ancient Romans invented the aqueduct and amphitheater but Italy gave the world the *Mona Lisa* and *David*; Dante's *The Divine Comedy*; the Verdi and Puccini operas; the plays of Nobel Prize winner Luigi Pirandello; the novels of Alberto Moravia, Italo Calvino, Umberto Eco, and Elsa Morante; and the films of Federico Fellini, Bernardo Bertolucci, and Liliana Cavani.

For more than 300 years, people from all over the world have flocked to Italy to see its art treasures, including 30,000 Roman Catholic churches and 20,000 castles. Many well-known novelists and poets, escaping to Italy from their own more conservative cultures, have written eloquently about their experience: Charles Dickens, Henry James, Mark Twain, Herman Melville, E. M. Forster, D. H. Lawrence, John Keats, Percy Shelley, Lord Byron, Goethe, and John Milton.

ART HISTORY IN MODERN LIFE

Millions of art lovers visit Italy to stroll in art museums in Florence, climb the steps of the Colosseum in Rome, marvel at Michelangelo's restored frescoes on the ceiling of the Sistine Chapel in the Vatican, and wonder at the magnificence of Leonardo da Vinci's original *The Last Supper* in Milan.

Italy is said to have more artistic masterpieces per square mile than any other country in the world. Many Italians see their country's art treasures every day without having to enter a museum. Examples of ancient and Renaissance architecture mingle with modern structures. Children play in piazzas crowned by ornate baroque fountains, and people worship in churches filled with art that is fit for the world's finest museums.

THE RENAISSANCE

In the entire history of Italian art (which continues in the present), the greatest contribution was made during the Renaissance, with enormous artistic and intellectual insights that brought the 15th and 16th centuries out of the obscure Middle Ages and put the ancient Greco-Roman civilizations, as well as Christianity, into totally new perspectives. The Italian Renaissance is traditionally divided into three main phases, or generations: Early, High, and Late.

The spirit of the Renaissance achieved its sharpest formulation in art, which was seen as a branch of knowledge capable of providing humankind with images of God and His creations and with insights into humankind's position in the universe.

The Sistine Chapel ceiling, painted by Michelangelo between 1508 and 1512, forms the cornerstone of High Renaissance art.

EARLY RENAISSANCE The Early Renaissance began in the early 15th century in Florence, where artists began to study the ancient Greeks and adopted their ideas about classical form and proportion. Renaissance artists portrayed the human body in an ideal or heroic manner, with a well-proportioned figure in a flattering position and showing emotion.

Filippo Brunelleschi (1377—1446) was the leading architect of this period. Using the classical Roman architectural principles of harmony and balance, he built the first Renaissance building, a hospital in Florence. His masterpiece, the dome of the Basilica di Santa Maria del Fiore cathedral, is considered the highest achievement of Renaissance architecture.

The sculptor Donatello (1386—1466) created beautiful, realistic statues of religious heroes, thus reviving the long-neglected style of the freestanding statue. Tommaso Cassai (1401—28), known as Masaccio, was the most notable painter of the Early Renaissance. He often derived his subject matter from ancient Rome, and his frescoes were remarkable for their use of perspective and their idealization of the human form.

The Santa Maria del Fiore cathedral in Florence had begun construction in 1296 in the Gothic style to a design by Arnolfo di Cambio and was completed in 1436 with the dome engineered by Filippo Brunelleschi.

Sandro Botticelli (1446—1510) is well known for his detailed painting *The Birth of Venus*, which depicts the goddess of love rising from the sea. Piero della Francesca (1416—92) filled his light-tone frescoes with graceful figures of exact proportions.

HIGH RENAISSANCE The High Renaissance, in the first part of the 16th century, was Italy's most creative artistic period, producing artists such as Leonardo da Vinci (1452—1519); Michelangelo di Lodovico Buonarroti Simoni (1475—1564); and Raffaello Sanzio (1483—1520), known as Raphael; and the architect Donato Bramante (1444—1514).

Artists were able to work on a grand scale due to the financial support they received from Italy's leading families such as the Medici of Florence and the Sforza of Milan. The Roman Catholic Church was also a great patron of the arts, wishing to fill the Vatican with important works of art and turn it into a magnificent monument to God. The colors and textures of the paintings of the High Renaissance are particularly dramatic, due to the use of oil paints rather than egg-based tempera.

Held in the Uffizi Gallery in Florence, Sandro Botticelli's celebrated 1486 painting, *The Birth of Venus*, uses Venus to portray the Italian Renaissance's ideal of beauty.

ART RESTORATION IN ITALY

Many of the world's masterpieces in Italy are in disrepair. Exposure to the climate and human activity has caused them to wear and tear, fade and flake. In the chapels, centuries of burning oil lamps and candles have coated the art on the walls with soot.

Massive efforts began in the late 20th century to try to restore Italy's art treasures to their past glory. Fine-art restoration has become a major profession, and there are schools that train people to become restorers of ceramics, paintings, buildings, and sculptures. Yet, even with the help of modern technology to map out in detail every inch of an original painting, restoration is still a painstaking and time-consuming effort.

Restorers took four times as long to restore The Last Supper *as it took da Vinci to paint it. The restoration effort, concluded in 1999, not only restored the colors dulled by humidity, dust, and pollution since the original was finished in 1498, but also repaired the damage done in previous restoration attempts.*

The Leaning Tower of Pisa began to lean soon after it was built in the 12th century because of sandy foundations. The tower continued to lean slightly more every year until in 1990, in danger of collapsing, the tower was closed. It took almost 12 years and $25 million to correct the incline of the centuries-old tower before it could finally be reopened to tourists in 2001. Now only 30 people are allowed to climb the tower at any time. The next step in the restoration project is to clean the tower's facade of grime.

Italians are concerned about the deterioration of their country's art treasures. In the major cities, vehicle emissions and movement have damaged many monuments. In Rome vibrations from road traffic have caused whole sections of marble to fall off some ancient monuments. In 1986 floods in Venice brought 5 feet (1.5 m) of water into piazzas, museums, and churches, soiling beautiful mosaics and paintings.

Unfortunately there are just too many art treasures in need of restoration for the national government to finance them all. Often, corporations and local governments donate money to support projects that are given priority.

One major restoration project that attracted a great deal of attention was the restoration of Michelangelo's frescoes on the ceiling of the Sistine Chapel. A Japanese television network, Nippon Television, donated $3 million to the project in exchange for exclusive rights to film the process.

As restorers cleaned away layers of soot from centuries of burning candles and the grease used by former restorers to impede cracking, the original colors of the paintings began to show. Contrary to the somber shades (deep grays, dark maroons, and earthy olives) and subtle shadows that Michelangelo's work had been known for, restoration revealed that the colors of his famous frescoes were loud and gaudy: neon purple, electric green and yellow, and glowing pink. Centuries of dirt had toned down the colors, giving them an earthy appearance.

Some art historians claim that the restorers went too far in their cleaning efforts—by removing the years of accumulated grime, they had also removed the dark shadows that Michelangelo had intended. According to Italian art critic Giovanni Carandente, "Michelangelo must be studied all over again, so revolutionary is this discovery about the painter of whom some had dared to write that in the Sistine he adopted colors that all leaned to brick or gray."

Da Vinci painted one of his finest works during the High Renaissance. *The Last Supper* depicts Christ's last meal, when he tells his disciples that he knows he will be betrayed. Da Vinci believed in "paint[ing] the face in such a way that it will be easy to understand what is going on in the mind" and so gave each of the disciples a different facial expression.

Bramante was commissioned by Pope Julius III to rebuild Saint Peter's Basilica in Rome, today the world's largest church. Many of the church's paintings and sculptures were done by Michelangelo. In his Sistine Chapel frescoes of God and Adam and his monumental sculptures of Moses and David, Michelangelo created powerful figures recognized by people around the world. While Michelangelo was painting the Sistine Chapel, Raphael painted several masterpieces on the walls of the papal rooms (now part of the Vatican museums). *School of Athens in the Stanza della Segnatura* is considered Raphael's greatest work.

The High Renaissance was represented in Venice by the painters Giorgione, Titian, Tintoretto, and Veronese and the architect Andrea Palladio, who built classical villas for the wealthy on the outskirts of the city and later inspired great international architects.

The Creation of Adam fresco on the ceiling of the Sistine Chapel was painted in 1511 by Michelangelo. It depicts the biblical story in which God breathes life, and creates the first man.

LATE RENAISSANCE During the latter part of the 16th century, a new style of painting, Mannerism, evolved. Mannerism refers to the highly stylized works of artists such as Pontormo and Parmigianino, who used strong colors and unnaturally elongated and emotionless figures, very different from the emotional, idealized subjects of earlier Renaissance painters. Mannerism was followed by the more elaborate baroque style in the early 17th century. Baroque definitively replaced the Renaissance esthetic ideal with a more dramatic, asymmetrical style. Noted baroque artists included Caravaggio, the Carracci family, and Bernini.

Raphael's *School of Athens*, in the Vatican, depicts Plato, Aristotle, and other great philosophers of ancient Greece.

THE OPERA

Italy has contributed tremendously to the development of Western music. European opera originated in Italy, and the Italian language provided the world with a musical vocabulary.

Musicians and poets in Florence began setting poems to music in the late 16th century. The first operas were produced in the early 17th century

FLORENCE—CITY OF CRAFTSPEOPLE

Many Italian cities and towns are renowned for their craftsmanship: Cremona in Lombardy for its master violin-makers; Carrara in Tuscany for its marble-cutters; Murano near Venice for its glasswork; and nearby Burano for its lacework.

However, the city of Florence is most associated with centuries of expert craftsmanship. Its narrow, winding streets are lined by tiny workshops where generations of artisans have perfected their fine skills. Certain workshops are devoted to silversmiths who create intricate figures and make jewelry to order. There are also woodcarvers who both carve items for sale and do expert restoration work in Florence's Renaissance churches. Metal sculptors, framemakers, and artisans also work in copper, bronze, and marble.

Many craftspeople in Florence work with leather and gold. Goldsmiths' workshops have historically been located in the buildings on Florence's oldest bridge, the Ponte Vecchio (below). There are even a few silk weavers who still work on a type of loom designed by Leonardo da Vinci. To create a length of fabric, the weaver threads each strand into the loom by hand; this is quite a job, since the pattern consists of 40,000 strands. Many silk weavers are women whose mothers and grandmothers also wove silk in the same workshop.

in Rome, Venice, and Naples. As the passion for opera swept the country, each city developed its own style. Claudio Monteverdi (1567—1643), considered the father of modern opera, led the Venetian school of composers. Alessandro Scarlatti (1660—1725) wrote nearly 100 operas and made Naples an operatic center. Leading European composers such as German-born George Frideric Handel (1685—1759) traveled to Italy to study opera. Even Mozart (1756—91) composed for Milan's La Scala, Europe's most famous opera house, which opened in 1778.

The original poster of Giacomo Puccini's opera, *Madama Butterfly*.

In 1816 Gioachino Antonio Rossini (1792—1868) composed the classic comic opera *The Barber of Seville*. Giuseppe Verdi (1813—1901), one of Italy's finest composers, wrote 26 operas, including *Rigoletto*, *La Traviata*, *Il Trovatore*, and *Aida* (set in Egypt and often performed with live animals such as camels). Known for their dramatic plots, his operas often dwell on the struggle of the oppressed. Giacomo Puccini (1858—1924) was another major 19th-century composer. His *La Bohème* and *Madama Butterfly* are well loved for their romantic, moving stories and melodies.

Opera first catered to the upper classes. Later, the opening of the first public opera house in Venice, in 1637, made it a source of entertainment for everyone. Crowds filled the halls on the opening night and discussed the performance for days after. Even today, Italians may talk during the performance; some get very involved with the action on stage and offer their comments to others around them.

LITERATURE

Before the 13th century, Italian writers composed in Latin, the formal language for literary purposes. In the 13th century, a group of poets at the court of Frederick II started writing in Tuscan, the dialect of Florence. Among

The Italian comic opera, or *opera buffa*, originated in Naples in the 18th century. It developed from the interludes that were performed between acts in serious operas.

the most famous writers of this time was Dante Alighieri (1265—1321) whose three-part poem, *The Divine Comedy*, has greatly influenced Italian literature. *The Divine Comedy* is an epic poetic work describing the journey through hell, purgatory, and heaven. The poet adopts a different voice in each part to match the mood of the place he is describing. Along the way he meets the souls of both the sinners and the saved and, threatened by both sides, illustrates the difficulty of choosing the right path.

The Divine Comedy also discusses important issues such as politics and its evils, various kinds of love, the nature of free will, and religious salvation. The work is an amazing exhibition of the length and breadth of Dante's knowledge and an important historical document about the Middle Ages.

Together with Dante, two writers marked the beginnings of Italian literature: Francesco Petrarca (1304—74), best known for his collection of Italian verses, *Canzoniere*, also called *Petrarch's Sonnets*, inspired by his love interest Laura; and the more entertaining Giovanni Boccaccio (1313—75), whose *Decamerone* (deh-kahm-meh-ROH-neh) is a collection of short, distinctly permissive, and realistic stories.

A fresco shows Dante holding a copy of *The Divine Comedy* next to the entrance to Hell.

THE ARTS IN MODERN ITALY

Italian artists continued to make a significant impact in the 20th century, when many avant-garde movements emerged throughout Europe. Nobel Prize-winning playwright Luigi Pirandello (1867—1936) and the writers Italo Calvino, Oriana Fallaci, Elsa Morante, Alberto Moravia, and Ignazio Silone have received international acclaim for their works.

Umberto Eco's novels—*The Name of the Rose*, a detective story set in a monastery in the Middle Ages, and *Foucault's Pendulum*, about the human condition—have sold millions of copies.

Other Italian artists include sculptor-painter Amedeo Modigliani, known for his elegant elongated portraits; surrealist painter Giorgio de Chirico; and opera singer Luciano Pavarotti.

Giorgio de Chirico's *Piazza d'Italia* was painted in 1952.

INTERNET LINKS

http://ec.europa.eu/culture/portal/sites/members/italy_en.htm

This website provides information about culture and arts in Italy, including visual arts, media, dance, books, and music.

www.uffizi.org

This is the official website of the famous Uffizi Gallery in Florence—a guide to what to see and how to buy tickets.

www.history.com/topics/italian-renaissance

This website provides information about the Renaissance period in Italy, including articles, videos, pictures, and facts.

LEISURE

Italians enjoy the simple things in life, such as eating a meal at a Venetian café and watching the world go by.

ITALIAN SUNDAYS are typically spent on leisure activities. Many Italians go to cafés, where they chat with old friends over coffee or wine, discuss politics, or argue passionately about the strengths and weaknesses of local soccer players.

Italian cafés allow, even encourage, their customers to stay as long as they like. Customers can read quietly, write letters, or meet friend after friend at the same table for hours without feeling any pressure to leave.

If it is a fair Sunday, an Italian family may enjoy an extended lunch at an outdoor restaurant, talking about how good the food and wine are, and, more importantly, discussing a variety of topics. Young Italians meet their friends at the local beach or a piazza in the city to just hang out.

In the heat of the day, some Italians enjoy taking a nap during their leisure time. They also spend time with friends and family, eating and shopping.

Gondoliers in Venice relaxing over a chess game during their free time.

THE PASSEGGIATA

The *passeggiata* (pah-say-JAH-tah), or evening stroll, is one of Italy's most enduring, civilized leisure activities. Every evening before dinner in many towns, people dress up and stroll in the main square, greeting one another as they meet and chatting amicably about the day's events. Some sit near the sidewalks at cafés and watch passersby.

The *passeggiata* gives Italians a chance to look their best and to see their neighbors dressed up as well. It is an avenue for them to touch base with fellow members of the community and to catch up on what has been going on in their neighborhood.

SOCCER MANIA

A passion for *calcio* (KAHL-choh), or soccer, is the strongest factor unifying Italy's competing regions. For some Italians, a Sunday begins at the church, after which the family has lunch together and then gathers in front of the television set to watch a soccer match.

Soccer is more than a sport or a business in Italy. Some fans may say that it is a part of living, like breathing! Of the three concerns most important to many Italian men (women, food, and soccer), the last takes precedence on the day of a big game.

Soccer was introduced to Italians in the late 1800s by the British, but it was not until the 1930s, under Mussolini, that the sport took off on an international level. Mussolini believed that a great Italian soccer team would be a source of national pride, and he saw to it that stadiums were built and teams nurtured all over the country.

Italy has had championship-winning teams ever since and has won the World Cup four times, the last time in 2006. In recognition of Italy winning the World Cup for a fourth time, all of the players were honored with the Italian Order of Merit of *Cavaliere Ufficiale*. However, at the 2010 World Cup in South Africa, Italy finished in last place in their group, losing to Slovakia. This was a shock to soccer fans in Italy and across the world because it was the first occasion when Italy failed to secure a victory in any game.

Italian children start playing soccer at an early age. A game can start anywhere—in a public square, on a small street, in the schoolyard—and at any time. Italians follow the big soccer leagues with passion. There are 16 Series A, or First Division, teams that play one another for the national title. The winner plays other national teams in European and international games. Soccer stories dominate the headlines of Italy's three sports daily newspapers—*La Gazzetta dello Sport*, *Corriere dello Sport—Stadio*, and *Tuttosport*—and its weekly sports magazine *Guerin Sportivo*.

Soccer fans supporting their team at a match. Italian soccer fans are passionately involved with the game and can reach heights of ecstasy or become absolutely despondent depending on whether their team wins or loses.

Italians are fiercely loyal to their city's soccer team. Some of the best Italian teams are Rome's SS Lazio and AS Roma, AC Milan (owned by Prime Minister Silvio Berlusconi), Turin's Juventus (owned by Fiat President Gianni Agnelli), and AC Fiorentina from Florence.

Italy's star players from past and present include Roberto Baggio, Paolo Rossi, Paolo Maldini, Dino Zoff, Salvatore Schillaci, Giuseppe Meazza, Marco Tardelli, Sandro Mazzola, and Gianni Rivera. Italy also imports some of the finest players from other countries.

The victories and losses of their favorite teams can make Italians very exhilarated or very angry. Italian soccer fans have a reputation for being rowdy and uninhibited in voicing their opinions about players, especially those not playing up to par. If a player gets hurt, fans are likely to call him "faker," "exaggerator," or even "old man." When the national team comes home from a World Cup defeat, fans are known to meet the players at the airport—not to help soothe their wounds, but to boo them! When a team wins, fans are likely to rush onto the field and rip the shirts off the players!

Soccer fans—in Italy called *tifosi* (te-FOH-se), which literally means "typhus carriers"—have been known to stir up violence at stadiums. One of the worst occurrences was at the 1985 European Cup, when 39 fans, mainly Italian, died in a brawl at the stadium in Belgium.

BASEBALL

Italians learned to play baseball from Americans stationed in Italy after World War II. Popular among Italian youth, the game is also played professionally, although Italian baseball professionals are not paid nearly as well as their counterparts on professional soccer teams, and the level of play is not up to that of American baseball. Many of Italy's professional baseball players come from the United States, some from the minor leagues and others as retirees from the major leagues.

Italian children enjoying a game of baseball as their parents watch from the sidelines.

Contemporary baseball in Italy has been likened to 1940s and 1950s baseball in the United States. Baseball stadiums in Italy are generally smaller and more intimate than those in the United States, and families bring picnic baskets to watch the game together. Many baseball games are held at the Stadio Steno Borghese, a baseball stadium built in 1991 and located in Nettuno, south of Rome.

The fans, like those for soccer, are extremely devoted and unhesitatingly vocal, but rarely violent.

BASKETBALL

Trained in soccer from an early age, Italian baseball players are said to play better with their feet than with their arms.

Basketball is fast gaining popularity among Italian children. Many watch the American NBA games on television, and some of the most devoted attend expensive basketball camps in the summer. Italian basketball players are often coached by Americans, and the best ones are sent to the United States to play on college teams with the promise that they will return to help the team at home. In 2006 Italy finished ninth in both the EuroBasket and World Championships. Sadly Italy failed to qualify for the 2009 EuroBasket tournament for the very first time since 1961.

OTHER OUTDOOR PURSUITS

Italians take part in amateur sports, such as horseback riding, running, cycling, swimming, boating, and tennis. During summer vacations, families rent beach or mountain cottages or go to their country villas. Skiing is popular in the winter months. There are ski slopes a few hours' drive from Rome, but the best skiing is found in the Italian Alps and the Dolomites. People living in small towns enjoy a relaxing type of lawn bowling called bocce.

The 2010 Formula One Italian Grand Prix held at the Autodromo Nazionale Monza racetrack.

Italians follow professional cycling and car racing with great interest. Italy's biggest cycling race is the Giro d'Italia, or "Tour of Italy." The annual competition, covering more than 2,000 miles (3,218 km), attracts the world's best riders. Italians have won the race a total of 67 times since the first race in 1909. The latest race in 2011 was won as runner-up by Michele Scarponi. Other Italians, including Marco Cipollini and Alfredo Binda, have made their mark by winning 42 and 41 victories each, respectively.

The Italian Grand Prix takes the Formula One race onto the Monza circuit 9 miles (15 km) northeast of Milan.

TELEVISION

Italians are avid television viewers. Television was introduced in 1939 but there are already 567 national digital television channels in Italy. The two main national television organizations are Radiotelevisione Italiana (RAI), which runs 15 channels, and Mediaset, founded by Silvio Berlusconi, which runs 16 channels, including Canale 5, Italia 1, and Rete 4. La7 is the third major network in Italy and newcomer Sky Italia, offering paid satellite TV programs, is gaining popularity. While Italian news, sports, and entertainment programs are traditional favorites, North American shows have become the rage. Italians love soap operas and game shows.

MOVIES AND MUSIC

Crowds of people gather to watch a performance at the world-renowned La Scala opera house (*Teatro alla Scala*) in Milan.

The golden year for Italian films was 1955 when people bought more than 800 million cinema tickets to see Italian-made Westerns (spaghetti Westerns) and epics. Ticket sales have since dwindled to fewer than 100 million a year, only about half the original number of movie theaters remain, and fewer movies are made every year.

Italians still love movies, but the teenagers—the ones who go to the cinema the most—seem to prefer Hollywood productions. Their parents, however, prefer watching movies at home to paying for the big-screen experience. To cater to the latter audience, some Italian directors make two versions of their films: one, a full-length feature film; the other, divided into episodes to fit the mini-series television format.

Italy's most famous directors include Roberto Rossellini (1906—77), Federico Fellini (1920—93), Franco Zeffirelli (*The Taming of the Shrew*, *Hamlet*), Bernardo Bertolucci (*The Last Emperor*), and Giuseppe Tornatore (*Cinema Paradiso*). Rossellini first gained international recognition in 1946 with *Open City*, while Fellini made his international breakthrough with *La Strada* in 1954.

Opera is big in Italy. Italians are serious opera lovers and feel proud to live in the country where opera was born. Venice, Naples, and Milan are the main centers, and there are free concerts of chamber or symphonic music in cities and towns throughout the year.

THE READING PUBLIC

Libraries and bookstores abound in many of Italy's cities but Italians generally do not read as many books as their northern European neighbors.

Italians, however, do spend a good deal of time reading newspapers and magazines.

Most of the nation's newspapers are published in the North, and each major city has one or two dailies with large circulations. Each major political party publishes a daily paper, as does the Vatican. Sports newspapers and magazines are extremely popular, as are illustrated weeklies that focus on women's topics, religion, politics, business, and popular culture. There are also numerous newspapers dedicated to Italian style in the areas of fashion, design, cuisine, wine, art, culture, and travel.

The writing style of many of Italy's most respected papers is said to be notoriously highbrow and directed toward the intellectual reader. Italian journalists tend to digress and do not hesitate to offer their own idiosyncratic opinions before describing the actual events. Many Italian newspapers have entire sections dedicated to literary and cultural issues, polemics, and criticism.

Elderly women in Venice.

The opening night at Milan's famous opera house, La Scala, usually in the first week of December, is one of the most exciting social and cultural events of the year. Opera lovers show up in black tie or long gowns, having bought their tickets weeks, sometimes months, in advance.

INTERNET LINKS

www.football-italia.net/
This is the news website for English-speaking fans of Italian soccer.

www.rai.it/
This is the official website of RAI, one of Italy's public broadcasting television and radio stations, with information on their programs.

www.italianculture.net/home.html
This website provides information about various cultural activities and events, including opera, music, art, and theater in Italy.

FESTIVALS

People enjoying the street tapestries created from flower petals during the Flower Festival, or L'infiorata, in Spello during Corpus Christi.

12

ITALIANS RELISH CELEBRATIONS, colorful parades and processions. The number of annual festivals in Italy is staggering; one takes place somewhere in the country almost every day. This is so even after the government decided in the 1970s that there were too many festivals and abolished seven, including Saint Valentine's Day.

There is a festival almost every month in Italy celebrating food, wine, music, art, religion, traditions, and much more.

Tradition is deeply ingrained in Italian culture. Italian festivals are mainly religious or historical. Many religious festivals honor saints. There are patron saints for different professions and special favors. Towns and villages also have their own patron saints and, on the saint's feast day, the inhabitants put on traditional clothes, play traditional music, and parade a large statue of the saint through the streets.

The historical festivals honor great events (many dating back to the Middle Ages or the Renaissance), on a national, regional, or local level. Such celebrations usually include a reenactment of the event, a costumed procession, and sometimes a mock battle or contest such as a horse race, ball game, or boat race.

FOOD AND THE ARTS

Italy is a gastronomic paradise in summer, with a string of food festivals. Some of these festivals celebrate ripening grapes; others celebrate eating truffles, making olive oil, or harvesting artichokes. Each town has

New Year's Day: January 1

Epiphany: January 6

Easter Monday: late March/early April

Liberation Day (national); Feast of Saint Mark (Venice): April 25

Labor Day: May 1

Republic Day: June 2

Feast of Saint John the Baptist (Florence): June 24

Feast of Saint Peter and Saint Paul (Rome): June 29

Assumption: August 15

All Saints' Day: November 1

Feast of Saint Ambrose (Milan): December 7

Immaculate Conception: December 8

Christmas: December 25

Saint Stephen's Day: December 26

The Judaeans' Feast is held during Holy Week in Messina.

its own specialty, such as strawberries in Nemi, mushrooms in Santa Fiora in Tuscany, calamari in Porto San Giorgio, tomatoes in Angri in Campania, roast pork in Ariccia, and wine in Montefiascone.

Some Italian festivals focus on the arts: opera, theater, film, poetry, or dance. Often guest performers are invited, even to arts festivals in small towns such as Palermo in Sicily, which hosts a famous puppet festival each year in November.

Italy's most famous arts festival is the Festival of Two Worlds in the Umbrian town of Spoleto. For three weeks in late June to early July, renowned dancers, musicians, and actors grace Spoleto's stages and streets. Cultural icons, such as Al Pacino, Yo-Yo Ma, Mikhail Baryshnikov, James Conlon, and Luca Ronconi have appeared at this festival.

THE IMPORTANCE OF FESTIVALS

Festivals unite Italians in a common purpose, reacquaint them with the past, and give them a sense of identity in the community. Before a feast day, the people of a town work together regardless of status to hang colored lanterns in the piazza, string tiny white lights on churches and monuments, plan fireworks displays, and set up long tables in the town square to hold food for the feast.

Locals of Marostica in Veneto dress up to watch the annual life-sized chess game during the La Partita a Scacchi con Personaggi Viventi Festival.

Families gather to make costumes and cook special meals. Workers take time off from work and soldiers from the army to take part in the festivities.

Before Corpus Christi every June, thousands in the medieval Umbrian town of Spello "paint" enormous, subtly colored replicas of such great works of art as Raphael's *Holy Family* and Michelangelo's *Moses* on the main street using flower petals. Some festivals are so elaborate that organizers begin preparing for next year's event as soon as the present year's ends.

To commemorate a chess game played by two noblemen in 1454 for the hand of a girl, the residents of Marostica, a medieval town in Veneto, turn the main piazza into a life-size chessboard in September every even-numbered year. The players stand on the board as chess pieces: the knights in armor ride horses, the king and queen wear royal robes, and the castles are floats wheeled by hidden drivers who practice their parts for six months before the game.

Carol Field, author of five award-winning books about Italian food, sums up the significance of festivals in *Celebrating Italy*: ". . . there are [country festivals] that celebrate asparagus, cherries, lemons, strawberries, apricots . . . ; festivals in honor of geese, frogs, ducks, and thrushes. . . . Festivals reenact the primal rhythms of the birth and death of seasons and crops, . . . the great release of warmth from the sun and of moisture from water that causes crops to be born. . . . Festivals are a key to the secrets of the world."

CARNIVAL

Carnival, or *carnevale* (kahr-neh-VAH-leh), which means "good-bye to the flesh," has been celebrated in Italy for centuries. Carnival is held during the 10 days leading up to Ash Wednesday, the first day of the season of Lent, which is a time of prayer, self-examination, and fasting in anticipation of Good Friday and Easter.

In the Middle Ages people wore masks and costumes to carnival balls, where they ate and drank excessively (the masks ensured anonymity and broke any sense of self-consciousness). During the 18th century, Carnival in Venice lasted six months.

Carnival is still celebrated intensely in a few cities in Italy, especially Venice and Viareggio. For 10 days, thousands gather in the Piazza San Marco, Venice's most famous square, in fair or freezing weather, to listen to music and to dance, dressed in elaborate masks and fancy costumes as knights, princesses, nuns, popes, or comedy (*commedia dell'arte*) characters. Other masks are based on more abstract motifs.

People in costume at the Carnival in Venice. Plays, masked balls, and fireworks are held in the city's streets and piazzas.

There are puppet shows, balls, operas, and drama productions. People caught in mock battles in the streets get hit by mounds of shaving cream. At the end of the festivities, a huge bonfire is lit, and an effigy of the King of Carnival is burned, indicating the end of the days of excess and the start of penitence and abstinence.

The Carnival of Viareggio on the Tuscan coast, officially celebrated since the 1870s, is famous for its seafront float parade. The floats, created by skilled artisans and fitted with sophisticated sound systems, are colorful, funny, and often satirical, parodying famous personalities.

PALIO DI SIENA

The *Palio* (PAH-lee-oh) *di Siena*, the biggest event in the Tuscan city of Siena, is a bareback horse race that originated in the early 14th century. The various

Celebrations during the week leading up to Easter include processions that reenact the life and death of Jesus Christ. In some towns, young men strike their legs with pieces of

cork studded with broken glass to experience a bit of the pain that Jesus Christ endured on Good Friday.

The Monday after Easter is a national holiday, often spent with the family at a picnic, if the weather permits. All who can make a pilgrimage to some grassy spot spread out a large picnic blanket and lay it with delicious food.

Easter Monday fare includes hardboiled eggs (symbolizing rebirth), sandwiches, pizza, lamb (representing innocence), salads, sweets, wine, and fruit. In Sicily people eat roasted artichokes, country bread, grilled lamb, and a grain dish. The Sicilian Easter sponge cake has layers of sweetened ricotta and candied fruit. Tiny lamb-shaped candies, chocolate eggs, and dough-covered, doll-shaped hardboiled eggs are other popular treats.

Sienese *contrada*, or districts, of the medieval Sienese republic compete in the *Palio*. Celebrated twice a year, in July and August, the race begins with a slow, dignified parade. Participants, dressed in medieval costumes of silk, fur, and velvet and bearing colorful flags and banners, represent the 17 *contrada*. The marchers make periodic stops, in front of important buildings along the route. The spectators, who number about 20,000, wave colorful scarves, indicating their allegiance to one of the medieval wards.

The solemnity of the 90-minute procession contrasts with the frenzy of the horse race that follows. Ten jockeys ride their unsaddled horses around Siena's magnificent Piazza del Campo. There are virtually no rules in the race, and a rider can do almost anything to win. He can strike another jockey or even give bribes. And he can claim victory even if his horse makes it past the finish line without him!

The winning horse-man team receives a banner with an image of the Virgin Mary, and they get to attend a jubilant feast the night after the race as honored guests.

CHRISTMAS

Italian families get together very often, but their gatherings take on a special meaning during the Christmas and Easter seasons. At Christmas the family sets up a small nativity scene in a prominent place in the living room. The nativity display may look more like a place in Italy than the town of Bethlehem where Jesus was born, and the figures in the creche may be dressed like Italians. The figures can be made from paper, clay, or stone, depending on the wealth of the family, and sets are passed from generation to generation.

The historic horse race at the Piazza del Campo of Siena in Tuscany.

Outside, the chilly streets of Italy's northern cities come alive in December: stores glitter with tiny white lights; wandering "shepherds" playing bagpipe-like instruments do their rounds; and street vendors sell roasted chestnuts.

Like North Americans, Italian families put up a Christmas tree in the living room. They also burn a yule log called *ceppo* (CHIP-poh) each night, and the children traditionally receive gifts on Christmas and on Epiphany. The second round of gifts comes from a kind old fairy called Befana. The presents go to the good children, of course, while those who have been naughty supposedly get coal and ashes.

Christmas brings back family members living away from home. On Christmas Eve the extended family gathers for a multicourse dinner that often centers on fish, with eel being the most important dish. (Fish markets in Italy display tanks of live eel during the Christmas season to entice shoppers.) During the family feast, the children sing carols and receive coins or praise from the older relatives. An ancient game similar to bingo follows the feast, and at midnight everyone attends Mass.

The whole family regroups on Christmas Day, after another Mass, for another grand dinner. This often starts with a very rich stuffed pasta served in broth, moves on to a still richer stuffed turkey or *tacchino*, and ends with traditional sweets that vary according to the region. Panettone is a fruit sponge cake familiar to all Italians at Christmas. The typical panettone is made with raisins and candied fruit, but each region has its own version. Some versions are coated in chocolate, others in toasted nuts.

Other Christmas treats include *torrone* (TOH-roh-nay), or nougat, *struffoli* (stroo-FOH-lee), or fried egg pastry coated with honey and colored sugar, and *panforte* (pan-FOR-tay), gingerbread made with hazelnuts and almonds.

Northern Italians generally enjoy larger feasts than many southern families, whose holiday dinners may consist of only fish dishes. (Some, however, serve 9, 13, or 24 courses.) In the South, the family feast is grander on Christmas Eve than on Christmas Day, while in the North it is the exact opposite.

A traditional Christmas nativity tableau at an Italian church.

INTERNET LINKS

www.festivaldispoleto.com

This is the official website of the famous Festival of the Two Worlds, with information relating to the program, press articles, sponsors, and box office.

www.venice-carnival-italy.com

This is the official website of the Venice Carnival, with information about its history, program, costume hire, and more.

www.2camels.com/festivals/italy.php

This website provides information on 55 fairs, celebrations, holidays, carnivals, and festivals of Italy, categorized according to the city or region.

FOOD

Gourmet food and wines sold at a store in Sicily.

13

Before eating a meal, Italians say "*Buon appetito!*" which means "Good appetite!"

TALIANS LOVE FOOD and consider good cooking an art. They are intensely proud of their traditional cuisine, which originated more than 2,000 years ago. Ancient Etruscan tombs were decorated with domestic scenes that showed cooking utensils, such as rolling pins and pasta cutters.

First- and second-century writers, such as Decimus Junius Juvenalis, who wrote several satires on many aspects of Roman society, and Gaius Petronius, whose *Satyricon* portrays the newly rich Trimalchio's dinner party, described in their accounts the kinds of food laid on the banquet tables of the wealthiest Romans. The menu included at least three courses—appetizer, main, and dessert—and often featured exotic meats, such as hare, gazelle, peacock, and even flamingo. Pike liver, sea urchin, oysters, stuffed wild fowl, and tender shoots of leek were other luxuries. Bread was served on silver plates.

Seafood, such as salmon, shark, lobster, and octopus were served to the rich, as well as goose and pheasant, milk and cheese, artichokes, celery, truffles, and radishes, and fruits, such as olives, figs, plums, cherries, dates, and grapes. The main dishes were elaborately prepared, using seasonings such as saffron, mint, vinegar, honey, and mustard.

Italians claim to have taught the rest of Europe to cook, and they are essentially correct. In the 16th century, Catherine de Medici brought Florentine cooks to France after she married King Henry. Today, Italian food is popular around the world. Spaghetti and pizza have been served

Fresh produce
fills this store
at a market in
Catania, Sicily.

"At the table, no
one grows old."—
old Italian proverb.

in the United States for so long that many think of them as American. Few people know that Italy is also responsible for introducing the world to ice cream, coffee, French fries, and fruit pies.

Italian cooking has also been influenced by other cuisines. The cooking in Sicily is said to be Greek in origin and Sardinian food has Phoenician roots. The northeastern Italian cuisines show Austrian, Hungarian, and Slovenian influences. Some even claim that Marco Polo, the Venetian explorer, brought pasta to Italy from China.

GROCERY SHOPPING

Fresh ingredients are essential to most Italian cooks. Many homemakers shop daily for the freshest meat, fruit, and vegetables. There is an open market in each village or town, and several in each city. Some of the stalls in these markets have been run by the same family for generations.

In Rome every neighborhood has a small market where residents can buy fresh seasonal produce. The larger markets are colorful, bustling places. Some stalls sell fresh, fragrant fruit and vegetables such as plump red tomatoes, wild strawberries, and Italian blood-red oranges. Others offer fish direct from the sea such as swordfish, tuna, eel, squid, and octopus. Still others have herbs, dried and fresh beans, wild mushrooms, breads, olive oils, and cheeses. Butchers sell sausages of all sizes as well as cuts of pork, lamb, and veal.

While shopping for ingredients, people can stop at stalls selling prepared foods for a snack: a slice of pizza, a ham or cheese sandwich, or a bowl of hot, homemade soup.

Aside from open markets, Italians also shop for groceries in large supermarkets, or *supermercato*, complete with convenience foods such as dried pasta, sliced bread, and canned and frozen foods.

There are also small stores licensed by the government to sell specialty items: the *panetteria* (pah-nay-teh-REE-ah) sells bread, rolls, and other freshly baked foods; the delicatessen, or *salumeria* (sah-loo-meh-REE-ah), sells items such as sausages and cheeses; milk, yogurt, and some cheeses can be purchased at the milk bar or *latteria* (laht-tuh-REE-ah); beef, veal, and poultry at the butcher's or *macelleria* (mah-cheh-luh-REE-ah); fish at the *pescheria* (pes-keh-REE-ah) or fishmonger's; fresh fruit and vegetables at the *fruttivendolo* (froot-te-VEN-doh-loh) or greengrocer; and canned goods at the convenience store, or *alimentari* (ah-lee-men-TAH-re). Shopping in the small stores takes time, but many Italian homemakers prefer to do so for fresher, tastier food and for a chat with the store owners. Urbanites often buy roast chicken and other prepared dishes at a *rosticceria* (ro-sti-chay-REE-ah), or "cookhouse."

This *salumeria* in Bologna features an extensive variety of cured meats and cheeses.

REGIONAL SPECIALTIES

Italian cooking is wonderfully diverse and creative. Just as each region of Italy has its own dialect, so too does it have its own special dishes and styles of cooking. In the past corn and rice formed the base for the northern Italian diet, while southern Italians ate primarily pasta. However these staples are no longer so strictly defined geographically. Pasta served in the North is generally flat, such as *capelli d'angelo* (kah-PEH-lih DAHN-jeh-loh) and linguine, while that served in the South is tubular, such as penne and macaroni. Northern Italians tend to cook with butter, while Southerners use olive oil.

Italian cooks prefer to use ingredients grown locally, and each region is famous for its specialties, cooked using traditional methods. The best egg pasta, Parmesan cheese, and prosciutto, or thinly sliced cured ham, come from Emilia-Romagna; the freshest fish dishes and flakiest pastries from Sicily; and the tastiest rice dishes from Veneto.

Italian cooking has been influenced by other cuisines. The cooking in Sicily is said to be Greek in origin, and that of Sardinia Phoenician. The northeastern cuisines show Austrian, Hungarian, and Slovenian influences. Some claim that Italian pasta was brought from China by Marco Polo, the Venetian explorer.

The *risotto alla milanese* is often made using arborio rice, a beef broth, cheese, and saffron.

Many of the major cities are known for a particular dish: Rome for the choicest roast lamb, Milan for the richest minestrone soup, Genoa for the most authentic gnocchi dumplings and pesto sauce, Naples for its pizza, Florence for its beef dishes, and Bologna for its lasagne and mortadella, or sausage flecked with bits of fat.

Italians are generally conservative in their food preferences and protective of their culinary traditions. In 1986, the opening of Italy's first McDonald's restaurant in Rome caused an uproar. Food purists protested outside the restaurant, giving away free spaghetti to remind Italians of their culinary heritage.

Today that McDonald's outlet is one of the world's busiest, and there are almost 300 outlets throughout the country, employing thousands of people. But some Italians have not forgiven its intrusion into Rome's historic district. A nonprofit movement calling itself Slow Food (with a snail for its symbol) tries to persuade Italians to preserve the art of dining, of making meals a leisurely and pleasurable experience. Slow Food is an international movement founded by Carlo Petrini in Italy in 1986. The movement seeks to preserve traditional cooking and cooking methods as an alternative to fast food. Members are encouraged to plant their own seeds and rear their own animals. Despite its small beginnings in Italy, it is estimated that there are more than 100,000 members in more than 150 countries today.

RISOTTO IN THE NORTH In the northern provinces of Lombardy, Piedmont, and Veneto, a rice dish called risotto replaces pasta at lunch and dinner. To make basic traditional risotto, rice from the Po Valley is boiled in a little homemade broth. As the rice absorbs the liquid, the cook adds a ladleful of broth and stirs the mixture. This is repeated a few times for about 20 minutes until the rice is plump. Then the cook adds butter, freshly grated Parmesan cheese, and saffron.

Sometimes other ingredients such as chicken, shrimp, sausage, ham, liver, herbs, vegetables, beans, and mushrooms are added. The regional dish of Venice is risotto made with peas. Very special risotto dishes are made with white truffles or black squid ink. Just as perfect pasta is served al dente, which means "firm when eaten," perfect risotto must be served *all'onda* (ahl OHN-dah), which means "rippling" or "in waves."

PASTA IN THE SOUTH Pasta forms part of the daily diet of southern Italians and many northerners as well. Pasta was commonly eaten with honey and sugar; tomato sauce was not added until the 17th and 18th centuries. Pasta was originally eaten using the fingers. One would simply pick up a few strands or pieces, tilt the head back, and gently lower the pasta into the mouth. Pasta was traditionally handmade by the mother of the household, who passed her techniques down to her daughters.

A versatile staple of traditional Italian cuisine, pasta comes in various types and sizes, which are usually a reflection of the locale from which they originated.

The Arabs brought dried pasta to Italy in the 13th century, and pasta has been part of the Italian's daily diet since the 15th century.

Amazingly enough there are more than 500 different varieties of pasta eaten in Italy today, all made with the simple ingredients of flour, water, and sometimes eggs. Traditionally the poorer southern Italians made pasta with just flour and water; only the Northerners could afford eggs.

The names and shapes of some types of pasta reflect Italians' creativity and sense of humor: spaghetti means "little strings," the thinner *capelli d'angelo* means "angels' hair," the flatter and wider linguine translates as "little tongues," and the ridged, tubular *sedani* (SAY-dah-ne) are "celery stalks." There are other kinds of pasta called "little mustaches," "little ears," "bowtie," "greedy priests," "priest stranglers," and "car-door handles."

The method of cooking pasta and the choice of sauce should suit its shape, length, and thickness. Thin noodles are best served with a light dressing, while thicker ones go well with a heavier cream or tomato sauce. Little shells and elbow macaroni are perfect for soups, while larger shells and macaronis, such as rigatoni, are best baked stuffed with cheese.

PIZZA FROM NAPLES Pizza's true home is Naples, where pizza chefs apprentice for two to three years before earning their qualifications. Classic Neapolitan pizzas include the cheeseless pizza marinara, using oregano, tomato sauce, and large hunks of garlic. Margherita pizzas are made with tomato sauce, local cheeses, and basil. (The latter is named for Queen Margherita of the House of Savoy, who praised it while visiting Naples in 1889.) Both pizzas are drizzled with olive oil before being baked for only two minutes in a large wood-fired oven, shaped like an igloo.

Other less traditional Neapolitan pizzas include the *quattro stagioni* (KWA-troh stah-JOE-neh), or "Four Seasons," made with mozzarella cheese and separate sections of mushrooms, seafood, anchovies, and capers, and *pizza alla pescatora* (pes-kah-TOH-rah), made with a combination of seafood, such as clams, squid, and shrimp. Neapolitans in a hurry buy fried pizza snacks, cooked in hot oil, from street vendors.

Raw and baked pizzas in Italy. Invented in Naples, the best pizzas are usually baked in a wood-fired oven.

ITALIAN WINES

Italy's wine history dates from classical times when the ancient Cretans called the Italian regions Enotria, the land of wine. Until recently only the famous Chianti, a red wine from the Tuscany region, was well known outside Italy. Yet, the vast Italian vineyards produce a fine variety of wines and make Italy the world's largest wine producer.

To guarantee the quality of its wines, the Italian authorities set strict regulations to control the production and pressing of the grapes and the aging and bottling of the wines. Bottles with a consistent quality of wine have DOC (Controlled Denomination of Origin) labels; only these wines are fit for export.

Italian wines have found their diversity in the country's numerous regional vineyards. The hilly areas of Tuscany, Friuli-Venezia Giulia, and Lazio are famous for their high-quality red wines, as are the plains of Lombardy and Emilia-Romagna. Liguria, Trentino-Alto Adige, and Veneto produce world-famous white wines. Italy's Spumante, a soft, mellow, sparkling white wine, is becoming well known and fashionable in the Italian home market. Like champagne, this wine is usually drunk on special occasions.

MEALS AND MEALTIMES

Most Italians eat three meals a day: a simple breakfast at about 8:00 A.M., a long lunch at 1:00 or 2:00 P.M., and a late dinner at about 8:00 or 9:00 P.M. Breakfast usually consists of coffee and bread or a roll. On the way to work, many city dwellers grab a quick breakfast at a café. They usually have a small cup of strong coffee and a sweet crescent roll.

Lunch, or *pranzo* (PRAHN-zoh), is the most important meal of the day. If possible parents and children come home to have a leisurely multicourse meal together.

As a rule, each course is served separately, and the plates are cleared before the next course. First may be an appetizer, or antipasto, literally meaning "pre-food." This often consists of a cold seafood salad, thin salami or ham slices served with melon; or artichoke hearts or mushrooms served with oil and vinegar. Often soup is served instead of antipasto.

The next course is a pasta or rice dish, followed by a main course of poultry, meat, or fish. Vegetables, salad, or cheese accompany the main courses, and bread is served throughout the meal. Fruit or a light sweet dessert is followed by coffee.

The evening meal is often similar to lunch and may be even more elaborate if there are visitors. Wine and mineral water are drunk at both lunch and dinner.

A typical Italian meal consisting of water, red wine, an appetizer, bread, soup, salad, and pasta.

GELATO

Italian ice cream is called gelato, meaning "frozen." Big cities have *gelate'ria* (jeh-lah-teh-REE-ah), or ice-cream parlors. Gelato may be served in thick slices cut from a *cas'sata* (kah-SAH-tah), a mound of various ice creams with chopped candied fruit and nuts. Flavors of gelato include *ciocco'lato* (choh-ko-LAH-to) or chocolate, *straccia'tella* (strah-chah-TEL-ah) or vanilla with chocolate chips, *nocci'ola* (noh-CHOH-lah) or hazelnut, *caffè* (kah-FEH) or coffee, *rum e uvetta* (rom-ill-VET-ta) or rum and raisin. Sherbet is made with peaches, strawberries, raspberries, melon, apples, kiwi, or bananas. Some parlors serve unusual flavors, such as champagne or avocado sherbet, or rice or celery gelato.

Italian ice cream is said to be lighter and tastier than North American ice cream. Good *gelate'ria* use only fresh ingredients, fresh fruit, or—for their coffee ice cream—freshly brewed espresso, in addition to the essential cream, sugar, and egg yolks. Tubs of fresh ice cream are displayed topped with pieces of fresh fruit and signs reading "homemade."

When it comes to preparing and eating exotic gelato, Italians are much more experimental than they are in trying a new pasta sauce. They do not hesitate to mix unlikely flavors in the same cup, and they are often eager to try the newest flavors or combinations at their favorite *gelate'ria*.

A neon-lit gelato parlour in Rome. Italian gelato differs from traditional ice creams as they are usually lighter, with a lower level of butterfat.

COFFEE

Italian coffee is always made from freshly ground beans, usually very strong. But there are many ways Italians like their coffee:

Espresso *senza schiuma* (SEHN-zah SHYOO-mah) is a small cup of strong coffee without foam on top, while espresso *con molta schiuma* (kon MOL-tah SHYOO-mah) is strong coffee with a lot of foam.

Espresso *lungo*, a "long" coffee, is a slightly larger cup of coffee that takes longer to drink, while espresso *al volo* (ahl VOH-loh), coffee "in flight," is a regular espresso served up quickly for someone in a hurry.

Espresso *macchiato* (mah-CHEEAH-toh), "spotted" coffee, has a drop of milk in it, while espresso *corretto* (koh-REH-toh) has a bit of alcohol added. Espresso *al vetro* (ahl VEH-tro) is served in a glass rather than a cup. (Some Italians think it tastes better this way.)

Cappuccino is coffee with hot, foamy milk. Cappuccino is served on ice, warm, or very hot. It may be "light," with a good amount of milk, or "dark," with just a little milk.

Caffè latte (LAH-teh) is coffee with an equal proportion of milk.

Some Italians enjoy sitting at a café table for hours, while others prefer to drink their coffee quickly and while standing. In Italy you pay about half the price if you stand and drink your cup rather than slowly sipping it at a table. Many Italians simply stand around the coffee bar, chatting with other customers while balancing their cup of coffee in one hand and a sweet roll in the other.

Coffee machines at a café in Oneglia, in the province of Imperia. Coffee had spread from the Muslim world to Italy through the thriving trade between Venice and North Africa, Egypt, and the Middle East.

The first Westerners to import coffee were the Venetians in 1615. The first Italian cookbook was written in 1474 by Bartolomeo Sicci.

INTERNET LINKS

www.italianfoodforever.com/

This website provides recipes, kitchen resources, and a food blog on Italian foods.

www.lagazzettaitaliana.com/italian-food-american-history.aspx

This website contains a brief history of Italian food in America.

www.italianmade.com/

This site is about food and wine made in Italy, including information about producers, eating in Italy, and the history and authenticity of food.

GNOCCHI WITH GORGONZOLA

(Makes 4 servings)

2.3 pounds (1 kg) floury potatoes

2½ cup (625 ml) all-purpose flour

1 egg, lightly beaten

3 cups (750 ml) Gorgonzola cheese

2 tbsp (30 ml) butter

3 tbsp (45 ml) double cream

pinch of black pepper

chopped chives, to garnish

Preheat the oven to 356°F (180°C). Put the unpeeled potatoes in a large saucepan, cover with salted water, and bring to the boil. Simmer briskly for 15—20 minutes until tender, then drain. Peel and cut in quarters. Place on a baking sheet and put it in the oven to dry for about 5 minutes. Pass the potatoes through a mouli or coarse sieve set over a large bowl. Quickly stir in the flour and egg, and season with salt. When nicely blended, cover with a clean tea towel to retain the warmth. Take a little of the potato mixture and roll into a long thin sausage. Slice into pieces about 1 inch (2.5 cm) long. Using a gnocchi paddle or a fork, roll the gnocchi with your thumb. Roll it the other way to make ridges on the side. Continue until you have used up all the potato mixture. Place the prepared gnocchi on well-floured trays as you work. Meanwhile bring a large pan of salted water to the boil. Drop in the gnocchi in batches. Simmer briskly for about 5 minutes until they rise to the surface. Drain gently using a wire scoop, and transfer to a warm serving dish. While the gnocchi are cooking, melt the Gorgonzola and butter in a saucepan over medium-low heat. When completely melted add the cream and boil for 1 minute. Add the cheese mixture to the gnocchi and gently stir to mix. Sprinkle with chopped chives and serve immediately.

TIRAMISU

(Makes 4 servings)

3 eggs, separated

½ cup (125 ml) caster sugar

1 cup (250 ml) mascarpone

7 ounces (200 g) Savoiardi ladyfinger biscuits, or sponge fingers

¾ cup (180 ml) espresso coffee dissolved in ¾ cup of hot water, left to cool

1½ tbsp (22.5 ml) bitter cocoa powder

berries and small sprigs of mint, to decorate

Whisk the yolks and sugar together in a large bowl. Add the mascarpone and continue whisking until the mixture becomes a very firm cream. In another large bowl, whisk the egg whites until firm and gently fold into the mascarpone cream. Dip the Savoiardi biscuits in the coffee and turn them to soften the other side. Take four cappuccino cups and put a layer of savoiardi in the bottom of each, breaking them into shorter pieces if necessary. Spread some of the mascarpone mixture over the top, and then repeat the layers two or three times to fill the cups. To finish, dust with cocoa powder and decorate with berries and sprigs of mint.

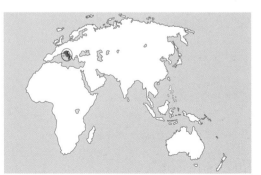

ECONOMIC ITALY

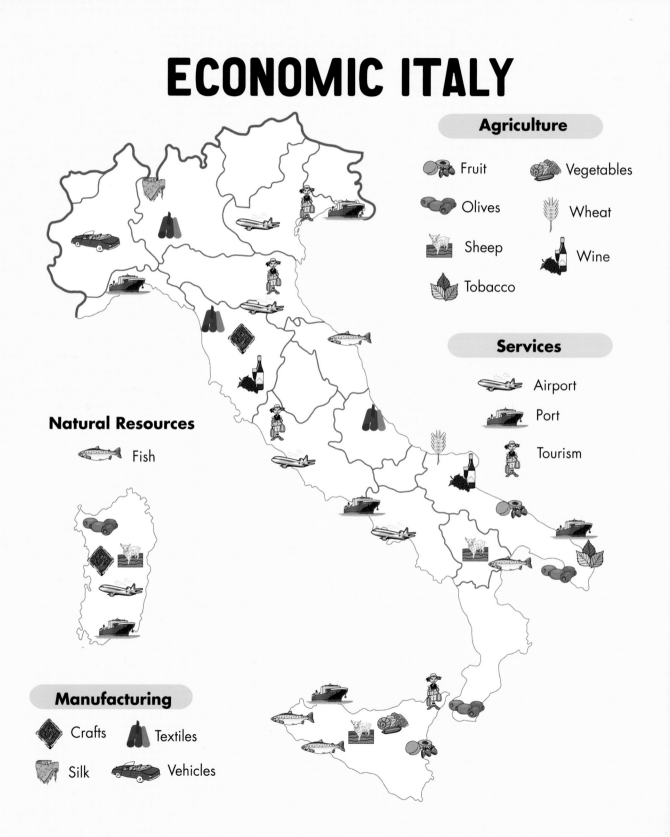

Agriculture

- Fruit
- Vegetables
- Olives
- Wheat
- Sheep
- Wine
- Tobacco

Services

- Airport
- Port
- Tourism

Natural Resources

- Fish

Manufacturing

- Crafts
- Textiles
- Silk
- Vehicles

ABOUT THE ECONOMY

OVERVIEW

Italy is the third largest economy in the Eurozone. However, it is in its fourth recession since 2001 and Italy has the European Union's second-biggest debt after Greece. Austerity measures have been passed in an attempt to reduce the public debt—value-added tax hikes, cuts to public spending, and pension reforms. The government has also embarked on wide-ranging structural reforms to boost productivity and potential growth. In spite of these measures, Italy's aging population, low trend productivity, low birth rates, and increasing unemployment is straining its ailing economy.

GDP

$2.1 trillion (2012 estimate)
Per capita: $30,100

GDP SECTORS

Agriculture 2 percent, industry 24 percent, services 74 percent

CURRENCY

The euro (EUR) replaced the Italian lire (ITL) in 2002 at a fixed rate of 1,936.27 lires per euro.
1 euro = 128 cents
USD 1 = EUR 0.78 (September 2012)
Notes: 5, 10, 20, 50, 100, 200, 500 euros
Coins: 1, 2, 5, 10, 20, 50 cents; 1, 2 euros

LAND USE

Arable land 27.9 percent, permanent 7.1 percent, forests and woodland 41.6 percent, artificial 4.9 percent, wetlands 0.2 percent, water 1.1 percent, other 17.2 percent

AGRICULTURAL PRODUCTS

Fruit (especially grapes), potatoes, sugar beets, soybeans, grains, olives, beef, dairy products, fish

INDUSTRIAL PRODUCTS

Engineering products, transportation equipment, energy products, minerals and nonferrous metals, tobacco, food products, beverages, textiles and clothing, footwear, ceramics, motor vehicles, machinery, iron and steel, chemicals

LABOR FORCE

25 million (2012 estimate)

LABOR DISTRIBUTION

Agriculture 3.9 percent, industry 28.3 percent, services 67.8 percent

UNEMPLOYMENT RATE

11.6 percent (2013 estimate)

INFLATION RATE

3.6 percent (2012 estimate)

MAJOR TRADE PARTNERS

China, Germany, France, the Netherlands, Spain, the United States, the United Kingdom

TOTAL EXPORTS AND IMPORTS

Exports: $484 billion
Imports: $524 billion (2012 estimate)

CULTURAL ITALY

Fashion capital

Milan Fashion Week showcases collections by the world's top designers. Via Montenapoleone, Via Sant' Andrea, and Via delle Spiga are the main fashion streets lined with designer boutiques like Gucci and Armani.

Silk city
Como's silk industry began in the mid-1600s and today produces more than 70 percent of the country's silk. The two most prominent families in the business supply fabrics to big fashion houses such as Versace, Dolce & Gabbana, and Trussardi.

Bridge of Sighs
Visitors to Venice can ride a gondola under the Bridge of Sighs to the sound of church bells from Saint Mark's Square. The bridge over the Rio di Palazzo, built in 1600, was supposedly named after the sighs of prisoners walking to the execution chambers.

Opera festival
Built in the first century A.D. and capable of seating 22,000, the Arena of Verona hosts an annual opera festival featuring world-class performances such as Verdi's *Aida*, Puccini's *Tosca*, and Bizet's *Carmen*. Shakespeare set *Romeo and Juliet* in Verona.

Leaning Tower

Pisa is home to the 12th-century building that continues to lean more each year.

Palio
During Siena's horse races in July and August, jockeys ride at breakneck speed around the main square, the Piazza del Campo, to win the Palio banner for their neighborhood.

Michelangelo's David
Florence's statue of *David* stands over 14 feet (4.3 m) tall at the Gallerie dell' Accademia. Michelangelo sculpted David as the symbol of a small but brave city and the model of the ideal Renaissance man, who relied on his own strength and courage to defeat a giant.

Colosseum

Inaugurated by Titus in A.D. 80, Rome's first permanent amphitheater covers about 261,360 square feet (24,281 square m), rises about 158 feet (48.5 m) high, and can seat 50,000 spectators.

Vatican City
The center of the Catholic faith, which is professed by about a billion people around the world, the Vatican is also the world's smallest state. Swiss Guards at the entrances to the city protect the Pope. Saint Peter's Basilica, completed in 176 years, towers with its dome that reaches more than 400 feet (122 m) above the ground. The *Creation* frescos on the ceiling of the Sistine Chapel were painted by Michelangelo.

Abruzzo National Park

This 234-square mile (606-square km) park contains forests of beech, pine, oak, maple, and other trees and animals such as the previously endangered Marsican bear and Apennine lynx.

Mount Etna

Despite being Italy's most active volcano, Mount Etna is still a big tourist attraction. Visitors walk along its craters, and souvenir shops, set up on its slopes, sell carvings made from the lava. Etna is a magnificent view at night as it spits fire into the sky.

Ancient ruins
Syracuse is home to impressive ancient ruins, such as the Temple of Apollo, Sicily's oldest Doric temple. The Archaeological Park preserves buildings from as early as 475 B.C., such as the Greek Theater, where Greek plays are still staged in May and June.

OFFICIAL NAME
Italian Republic

NATIONAL FLAG
Three equal vertical bands: green, white, and red. Inspired by the French flag that Napoleon brought to Italy in 1797.

NATIONAL ANTHEM
Fratelli D'Italia (Brothers of Italy). Adopted in 1946. Words written by Goffredo Mameli; music composed by Michele Novaro.

CAPITAL
Rome

OTHER MAJOR CITIES
Bologna, Florence, Genoa, Milan, Naples, Palermo, Turin, Venice

ADMINISTRATIVE DIVISIONS
Abruzzi, Apulia, Basilicata, Calabria, Campania, Emilia-Romagna, Friuli-Venezia Giulia, Lazio, Liguria, Lombardy, Marche, Molise, Piedmont, Sardinia, Sicily, Tuscany, Trentino-Alto Adige, Umbria, Valle d'Aosta, Veneto

POPULATION
61,482,297 (2013 estimate)

LIFE EXPECTANCY
81.86 years (2012 estimate)

ETHNIC MAJORITY
Italian

RELIGIOUS GROUPS
Roman Catholic majority, established Protestant and Jewish communities, growing Muslim immigrant community

LANGUAGES
Italian (official), German (parts of Trentino-Alto Adige), French (Valle d'Aosta), Slovene (Trieste)

PUBLIC HOLIDAYS
New Year's Day (January 1); Epiphany (January 6); Easter Monday (March/April); Independence Day (March 17); Liberation Day (April 25); Labor Day (May 1); Republic Day (June 2); Feast of the Assumption (August 15); All Saints' Day (November 1); Feast of the Immaculate Conception (December 8); Christmas Day (December 25); Saint Stephen's Day (December 26)

FAMOUS RENAISSANCE ARTISTS
Giovanni Bellini, Sandro Botticelli, Donato Bramante, Filippo Brunelleschi, Michelangelo Buonarotti, Tommaso Cassai, Leonardo da Vinci, Donatello, Andrea Palladio, Raffaello Sanzio

OTHER LEADERS IN THE ARTS
Giacomo Puccini, Giuseppe Verdi, Luciano Pavarotti (opera); Amedeo Modigliani (painting); Dante Alighieri, Umberto Eco, Luigi Pirandello (literature)

TIMELINE

IN ITALY	IN THE WORLD

2,000–800 B.C.
Latins and Italics arrive, followed by Etruscans in 1200 B.C., and Greeks and Phoenicians in 800 B.C.

810 B.C.
Phoenicians establish Carthage.

509 B.C.
The first Roman republic is established.

272 B.C.
Rome conquers Italy.

116–17 B.C.
The Roman Empire reaches its greatest extent, under Emperor Trajan (98–17 b.c.).

146 B.C.
Romans destroy Carthage in the Punic Wars.

A.D. 600
Height of Mayan civilization

A.D. 800
The Holy Roman Empire is established.

1000
The Chinese perfect gunpowder and begin to use it in warfare.

1434
The Santa Maria del Fiore is completed with Filippo Brunelleschi's famous dome.

1478–80
War between Florence, Venice, and Milan, and the Papacy, Siena, and Naples

1495–97
Leonardo da Vinci paints *The Last Supper*.

1508–12
Michelangelo paints the ceiling of the Sistine Chapel.

1530
Beginning of trans-Atlantic slave trade organized by the Portuguese in Africa.

1558–1603
Reign of Elizabeth I of England

1755
Genoa sells Corsica to France.

1776
U.S. Declaration of Independence

1789–1799
The French Revolution

1796–97
Napoleon's army invades Italy.

1831
Birth of the Risorgimento movement

1861
The United Kingdom of Italy is proclaimed.

1861
The U.S. Civil War begins.

1870
Rome becomes the capital.

1869
The Suez Canal is opened.

IN ITALY	IN THE WORLD
	1914 World War I begins.
1915 Italy enters World War I.	
1925 Mussolini becomes dictator.	
	1939 World War II begins.
1940 Italy enters World War II on Germany's side.	
1944 Allied forces seize Rome.	
	1945 The United States drops atomic bombs on Hiroshima and Nagasaki.
1949 Italy joins NATO.	**1949** The North Atlantic Treaty Organization (NATO) is formed.
1957 Italy joins the European Community (EC).	**1957** The Russians launch Sputnik.
	1991 Break-up of the Soviet Union
1994 Silvio Berlusconi is investigated for corruption and resigns.	**1997** Hong Kong is returned to China.
1999 Azeglio Ciampi is sworn in as president.	
2001 Berlusconi becomes prime minister.	**2001** World population surpasses 6 billion.
2002 The euro replaces the lire.	**2003** War in Iraq begins
2008 Financial crisis affects world economy—Italy slides into recession. Berlusconi wins election.	**2009** Outbreak of flu virus H1N1 around the world.
2011 Berlusconi stands down as prime minister after scandals. Debt crisis continues.	
2013 Giorgio Napolitano, at age 87, is re-elected for a second term as president.	**2013** A devastating, mile-wide tornado touches down, leveling a suburb near Oklahoma City.

GLOSSARY

a braccetto (ah-bra-CHET-toh)
The way two men or women walk arm-in-arm, showing friendship.

antipasto
An appetizer of cold dishes served before the main course at lunch or dinner.

bocce
An Italian version of bowls played on a lawn smaller than a bowling green.

calcio (KAHL-choh)
Soccer, the national sport.

carnevale (kahr-neh-VAH-leh)
Literally "good-bye to the flesh," this great festival is celebrated for 10 days prior to Ash Wednesday, the beginning of Lent.

ciao (CHAOW)
An informal greeting that can mean either hello or good-bye.

commedia dell'arte (kom-MAY-diah del-LAHR-teh)
A style of popular comedy theater developed during the Renaissance.

gelato
A frozen dessert, such as ice cream and sherbet.

Giro d'Italia
Italy's biggest cycling marathon, which attracts cyclists from other countries as well and is celebrated by crowds and covered by the mass media.

la bella figura (lah BEL-lah fe-GOO-rah)
Literally "beautiful figure," this term refers to refined and cultured behavior.

Mezzogiorno (med-zoh-JOR-noh)
"Land of the Midday Sun"; indicates the southern regions of Italy.

panettone
A Christmas sponge cake, usually with raisins and candied fruit.

passeggiata (pah-say-JAH-tah)
An evening stroll in the neighborhood to socialize.

piazza
The town square.

Renaissance
The era of artistic and intellectual rebirth that lifted Europe out of the Middle Ages.

Risorgimento (ree-sohr-gee-MEN-toh)
Meaning "Resurgence," a 19th-century movement for Italian unification.

risotto
Rice boiled in broth, with butter and Parmesan cheese added; commonly eaten in northern Italy.

sciroc
A hot, dry wind that blows across Sicily and the southern Italian provinces in summer, it is laden with very fine red sand from the Sahara Desert in northern Africa.

FOR FURTHER INFORMATION

BOOKS

Alighieri, Dante, and Sisson, C. H. (translator). *The Divine Comedy.* (Oxford World's Classics). Oxford: Oxford Paperbacks, 2008.

Dunford, M. *The Rough Guide to Italy.* London: Rough Guides, 2011.

Gilmour, D. *The Pursuit of Italy: A History of a Land, its Regions and their People.* London: Allen Lane, 2011.

Hardy, Paula. *Italy (Country Guides).* London: Lonely Planet, 2012.

Kalman, Bobbie. *Spotlight on Italy (Spotlight on My Country).* New York, NY: Crabtree Publishing Company, 2011.

Matthew, John. *Foods of Italy (Culture in the Kitchen).* New York, NY: Gareth Stevens Publishing, 2011.

Petronius, and Walsh, P. G. (translator). *The Satyricon.* (Oxford World's Classics). Oxford: Oxford Paperbacks, 2009.

Throp, Claire. *Italy (Countries Around the World).* Chicago, IL: Heinemann-Raintree, 2011.

WEBSITES

BBC Country Profile, Italy. www.bbc.co.uk/news/world-europe-17433142

CIA World Factbook Italy. www.cia.gov/library/publications/the-world-factbook/geos/it.html

History for Kids. www.historyforkids.org/learn/medieval/history/highmiddle/italy2.htm

Italy Guides. www.italyguides.it/us/italy_travel.htm

Michigan State University: Italy. http://globaledge.msu.edu/Countries/Italy

National Geographic. http://travel.nationalgeographic.com/travel/countries/italy-guide/

Rough Guides. www.roughguides.com/travel/europe/italy.aspx

FILMS/DVDS

Best of Europe: Beautiful Italy. Small World Productions, 2010.

Brava Italia. Acorn Media, 2010.

Experience Italy. TravelVideoStore.com, 2008.

Francesco's Italy: Top to Toe. 2 Entertain, 2008.

MUSIC

Angelo De Pippa & The Italian Musica. *Legendary Favorite Songs of Italy.* Legacy International, 2009.

Banco del Mutuo Soccorso. *Banco del Mutuo Soccorso.* Sony/BMG Italy, 2010.

Eiffel 65. *Eiffel 65.* Universal, 2010.

Italian Favorites. Music of Italy, 2010.

BIBLIOGRAPHY

BOOKS

Caselli, Giovanni. *In Search of Pompeii: Uncovering a Buried Roman City.* New York: Peter Bedrick Books, 1999.

De Vacchi, Pierluigi, and Gianluigi Colalucci (contributor). *Michelangelo: The Vatican Frescoes.* New York: Abbeville Press, 1997.

MacDonald, Hamish. *Mussolini and Italian Fascism.* Pathfinder History Series. Cheltenham, United Kingdom: Nelson Thornes, 1999.

Pope John Paul II, and John Vitek (editor). *My Dear Young Friends: Pope John Paul II Speaks to Youth on Life, Love, and Courage.* Winona, MN: St. Mary's Press, 2002.

WEBSITES

Arts and Culture in Italy. www.bbc.co.uk/news/entertainment-arts-17337752

BBC News. http://news.bbc.co.uk/1/hi/world/europe/country_profiles/1065345.stm

Catholic churches in Italy. www.telegraph.co.uk/news/worldnews/1543643/Italian-church-attendance-lower-than-thought.html

Central Intelligence Agency World Factbook (select "Italy" from the country list). www.cia.gov/cia/publications/factbook

Embassy of Italy in the United States. www.italyemb.org

Food in Italy. www.nationmaster.com/graph/foo_mcd_res-food-mcdonalds-restaurants

Inflation in Italy. www.tradingeconomics.com/italy/inflation-cpi

Italian Information and Data. www.pressreference.com/Gu-Ku/Italy.html

Italian Ministry of Foreign Affairs. www.esteri.it/eng/index.htm

Italian Tourism. www.italia.it/en/home.html

Italian Soccer. www.serieaweekly.com/2009/06/top-italian-football-players-of-all-time.html

Italian Soccer Federation (FIGC). www.figc.it/versione_inglese/default.htm

Italy Travel Guide. www.justitaly.org/

Land Use in Italy. www.indexmundi.com/italy/land_use.html

Living in Italy. www.expatforum.com/articles/cost-of-living/cost-of-living-in-italy.html

Lonely Planet World Guide: Destination Italy. www.lonelyplanet.com/destinations/europe/italy

National Institute of Statistics. www.istat.it/English/index.htm

Papal Systems. www.answers.com/topic/how-many-popes-have-there-been

Religion in Italy. http://mg.co.za/article/2006-01-19-survey-shows-italians-tailor-religion-to-fit-their-lifestyles

The Roman Empire. www.roman-empire.net

U.S. Department of State. www.state.gov/r/pa/ei/bgn/4033.htm

INDEX

INDEX